Beau
A Ma

BEAUTY OF THE BEAST

A MAKEUP MANUAL BY EMILY SCHUBERT

	Introduction	**7**
	Preparing Yourself & Your Subject	**10**
	Skin Preparation	**12**
	Notes for Set	**13**
	Massage Technique	**14**
	Color Theory	**17**
	Check Your Color Vision	**18**
	Toolkit	**21**
	Notes on Removal	**25**
	Dead & Alive	**27**

CHAPTER 1a: ALIVE

SKILL	◊ HEALTHY	**31**
	◊ How to Sweat	**41**
	◊ How to Cover a Pimple	**41**
	◊ How to Apply a Tattoo	**42**
	◊ How to "Remove" a Tattoo	**44**
	◊ How to Cry with Mascara	**45**
LOOK	◊ ALIVE	**46**

CHAPTER 1b: DEAD

SKILL	◊ ILL	**53**
LOOK	◊ DEAD	**60**

CHAPTER 2: OLD

SKILL	◊ OLD AGE STIPPLE	**67**
	◊ How to Age Hair	**76**
	◊ How to "Remove" a Tooth	**76**
	◊ How to Age Nails	**77**
LOOK	◊ OLD	**78**

CHAPTER 3: YOUNG

SKILL	◊ SKIN MANIPULATION	**87**
	◊ How to Reverse Contour	**91**
LOOK	◊ YOUNG	**92**

CHAPTER 4: BALD		
SKILL	◊ BALD CAP	**101**
	◊ How to Cover Eyebrows	**112**
	◊ How to Create a Scar	**114**
	◊ How to Make a Fake Pimple Using a Bald Cap	**115**
LOOK	◊ BALD	**116**

CHAPTER 5: HAIRY		
SKILL	◊ BEARD & MUSTACHE LAYING	**125**
	◊ How to Blend Hairs	**131**
	◊ How to Create Stubble	**131**
LOOK	◊ HAIRY	**132**

CHAPTER 6: BONY		
SKILL	◊ PROSTHETIC APPLICATION	**141**
LOOK	◊ BONY	**148**

CHAPTER 7: BLOODY		
SKILL	◊ CUT	**157**
	◊ How to Make a Neck Bladder	**165**
	◊ How to Apply a Neck Bladder	**168**
	◊ Blood Types	**169**
LOOK	◊ BLOODY	**170**

	Glossary	**177**
	Suppliers	**178**
	Further Reading	**179**
	Colophon	**180**

INTRODUCTION

My career as a makeup artist did not begin on a movie set.

I was in a hospital bathroom at 13 years old. I had just received reconstructive back surgery for a severe case of scoliosis. When I caught sight of myself for the first time since the surgery, the pinkish hue that normally animated my face seemed to have vanished. I was in grayscale. Thinking it was a trick of the lighting, I pressed the button that opened the bathroom door, and, slowly, let in the daylight. Yet I remained gray—matching, I noticed, the tiles of the wall behind me.

Later I was told that during surgery I lost so much blood that half of my body's supply had been replaced with plasma. I was lacking hemoglobin: a protein in red blood cells that carries oxygen and gives life, color—blush—to your face.

My scoliosis and its aftermath caused other curious changes to my body. I developed a protrusion where one of my ribs grew out of my chest three inches. Other girls around me grew chest protrusions of their own, two, symmetrical for the most part. My situation needed correction; the surgeon straightened my spine along titanium rods, my ribs were broken and rearranged, and as a result I grew 4.5 inches overnight. High on morphine, I knew this: I had become a different kind of creature right before my eyes.

All of this to say, you and your body are not one and the same. Your body can betray you. It can be manipulated by forces outside your control, changed permanently. The marks on your body, its coloration, sun exposure, posture, the shape of your bones and your extremities, inherited or otherwise—all of this tells a story. It is your life's experiences writing on you, whether you like it or not.

That lesson led into another. If the body is so changeable, so open to manipulation, why not have a hand in the process? If only as a means of survival.

After weeks of feeling alienated at school, I found not confidence, exactly, but a particular kind of power. I began helping my friends get out of tests and assignments by making them look sick on purpose. I would meet them in the school bathroom and apply blush around their nose (as if raw from Kleenex use) and around their eyes (as if inflamed from sneezing). I smudged mascara under their eyes, as if they were suffering from exhaustion. My friends would tell their teachers they felt simply *awful*. They could take the test, but it wouldn't be their best. They got sent home.

When my big brother, whose friend was studying film in school, learned about my specialized skills, he got me a job on set. I was 14, and the assignment was to make a 9-year-old boy look like he had survived a zombie apocalypse. I came with my beauty makeup kit, not knowing what I was getting myself into. I took the black eye shadow I used for eyeliner and, with my fingers, applied it in between his ribs. This made them protrude out of his body—a familiar sight to me. For other characters who were supposed to look ill, I applied gray cream makeup to their faces, so they looked like I had in that hospital bathroom mirror.

◊ ◊ ◊

In your hands is a transformation manual.

Makeup is most often associated with beauty, and by extension, vanity. This book proposes something different. We will see makeup as a portal. On the other side lies any kind of character or creature you wish to inhabit or conjure in someone else—and, with the help of a camera, immortalize.

I have studied that alchemy for about half my life. This manual distills what I have pieced together over many years—my tricks of the trade—into one handy book.

Each chapter will identify a category of makeup and explain its role in the stories we watch on our screens. There will be tutorials and suggestions for how to use makeup to create a narrative. You will learn how to make someone look decades younger or older, deathly ill or radiantly alive, completely bald or covered with hair. Once you have studied these fundamentals, you will take on more advanced effects like bloody wounds and prosthetic application, all in the name of unbridled make-believe.

The techniques you will learn come from both professional beauty makeup and the world of special effects (SPFX). Beauty techniques will include facial sculpting and the selection of blush pigments. With SPFX, we will begin working three-dimensionally, expanding a nose or fabricating a pimple that is ready to pop.

With these lessons, we will exercise our imagination and touch, gaining knowledgeable use of the hands. We'll be discovering and trying to master an unusual skill set: painting and sculpture in motion. Not dissimilar to puppetry, you bring an object into existence and then step back, allowing someone else to operate.

I could, it's true, keep these tricks to myself, but I would rather see what you will do with them.

— Emily Schubert

PREPARING YOURSELF & YOUR SUBJECT

Before you begin, make sure all your materials and tools are laid out on a clean surface (a towel, for example) and are easily accessible.

Consider the lighting around your work table and mirror. If you're on set, keep in mind how the lighting of your workstation compares to the lighting on camera. If natural daylight is an option, arrange your workstation with the back of your mirror facing the window. When working in artificial light, the key consideration is to avoid creating shadows on your subject's face, which is why at least a two-source lighting rig (such as a ring light) is ideal.

Now, take a few moments to examine your subject. Use this time to get to know their face and its structure. Pay attention to shadows.

Begin by asking a question:

"Are you wearing anything on your face right now?"

Ask them what they like to highlight about their face. Do they like to wear lipstick or eyeliner? This will educate you on their personal makeup philosophy and practice and what kind of goals they have in the chair. Establishing an attitude of curiosity around your subject's preferences is important.

Your subject may reveal they have allergies during this conversation. If they don't, ask them.

Then ask:

"Can I use my fingers?"

Remember that makeup is one of few professions that involves laying your hands directly on another person's face. You must do so with authority and awareness.

Some makeup processes are likely to be lengthy or potentially uncomfortable. It is important to be clear with your subject about what you have planned for them and make time for breaks if necessary.

In many ways, the makeup artist serves as a portal. When working on a film set, the actor passes through your chair and it's up to you to take them out of themselves and into their character. By asking them the right questions before you begin, you can understand their stance on makeup and the transformation to come, as well as how they see your role in the process. There's always an opportunity for an indirect transferral of knowledge from makeup artist to actor, and vice versa.

SKIN PREPARATION

No matter what makeup you're applying, begin by cleansing the face with either micellar water or an astringent such as witch hazel. The former is best suited for beauty makeup and more sensitive skin, the latter for special effects applications. The witch hazel is important for prosthetics, for instance, because it removes any surface oils that might degrade the appliance. In either case, use two cotton rounds to apply the solution to both sides of the face in confident swiping movements (symmetry is key). This way, you begin work with a clean canvas.

For many of the skills you will learn in this book, applying a moisturizing layer is an essential next step. For the purposes of film, emollient creams are preferable, but for everyday beauty regimens you might use a simple oil at this stage. If you (and your subject) opt for oil, grapeseed oil is preferable, but remember that you will then need to avoid water-based makeup—you can layer oil on top of water, but never water on top of oil. Makeup application relies upon the interactions between products and materials, and this must be respected.

Apply moisturizer with a light lymphatic massage. This not only helps you standardize your process, but it also:

◊ Familiarizes your hands with your subject's face.

◊ Ensures an even, thorough application.

◊ Brings blood to the surface of the skin and drains excess lymphatic fluid.

◊ Relaxes your subject into the role they are soon to play. The massage provides them the space to leave their body momentarily and return as their character.

Remember: your hands are the most important tool in your toolkit.

NOTES FOR SET

◊ On film sets, always ask the cinematographer before using aerosols, sprays, or loose powders in front of the lens.

◊ Keep your tools and equipment clean, and sanitize between subjects. You will often find it beneficial not to clean your brushes during an application—the build-up of remaining product can be very helpful.

◊ While sponges are one of the most sanitary and effective ways to apply makeup, feel free to use your fingers when you're not moving back and forth between multiple subjects, as it wastes less product.

◊ Avoid scented products when possible, to avoid any allergic reactions (or personal associations the subject may have with the scent). If you're in a particularly noxious environment, you can dab a neutral, traditionally pleasant scent, such as lavender, on the inside of your wrists.

◊ Be discreet when considering acting aids like tear sticks—actors vary in their personal philosophy on this point.

◊ When makeup is completed and you are ready to go to set, always pack a set bag and/or belt with the products that you will need to do touch ups.

◊ Using SPF protection is crucial. Even when a sunburn is required of a character, you must protect the actor's skin and paint it in yourself.

MASSAGE TECHNIQUE

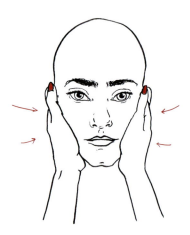

1 First, warm the moisturizer to your body temperature by applying a generous amount to your hands and coating them, front and back. Place both of your hands on your subject's face, pressing in an even layer of moisturizer and acclimating your hands to their facial contours.

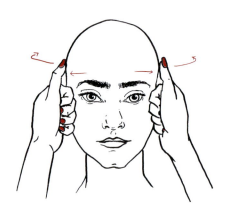

2 Place your middle knuckles on your subject's temples and knead with your thumbs in an outward motion starting at the center of their forehead toward their hairline.

3 Alternate one thumb steadily after the other. Press down to relieve tension in the forehead and stimulate lymphatic fluid.

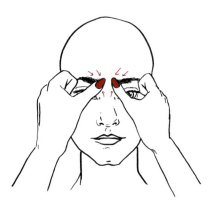

4 Now take your thumbs, hook them into the brow bone, and hold. If you feel a lot of tension, take the knuckles of your forefingers and rest them on top of the brow bone also—it should feel like you're holding all the tension between your forefinger and your thumb.

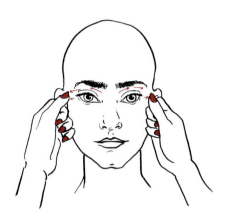 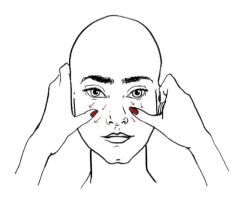

5   Extend the motion just under the brow ridge and land at the temples. Hold. Repeat with light pressure.

6   Move on to the undereye area. With one hand moving lightly behind the other, keep your hands moving in an outward motion in the area between the eyes and the nasolabial folds, tracing the orbital bone.

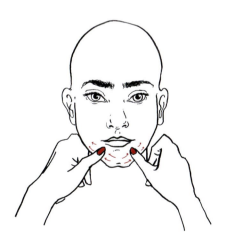 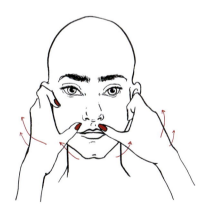

7   With the same motion, work down the face until you get to the chin. Press where you feel the most tension, usually under the cheekbones and/or around the TMJ muscle (the two joints that connect your lower jaw to your skull, in front of each ear).

8   Make some passes hooking your fingers under the jaw.

9 In one big symmetrical motion, trace your movements on the jawbone and apply pressure as you move down to the neck. This is the final lymphatic drainage step.

10 Using your knuckles, repeat the motion starting at the ears and moving down the neck on either side, landing at the clavicle. Hold, and apply pressure.

COLOR THEORY

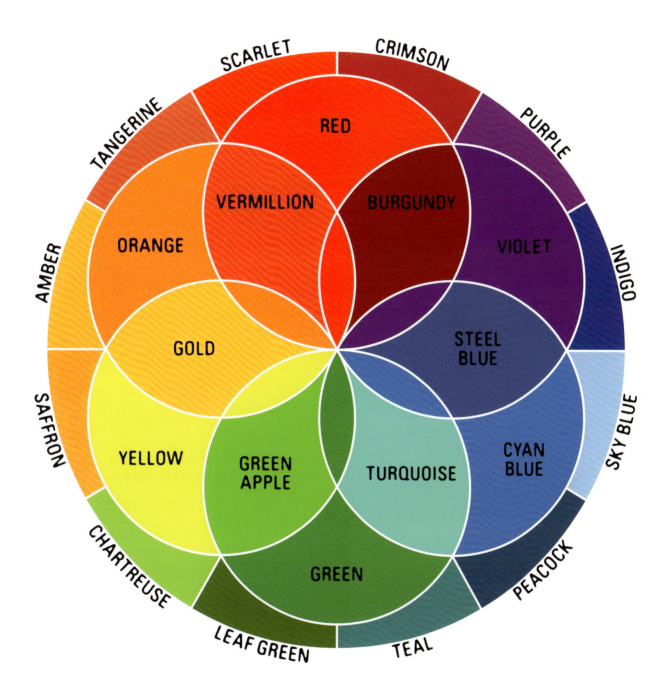

Use this color wheel as a reference for color correcting, as in Skills 1a, 1b, and 2.

CHECK YOUR COLOR VISION

What do you see? Test your color proficiency with the original Ishihara Color Blindness Test.

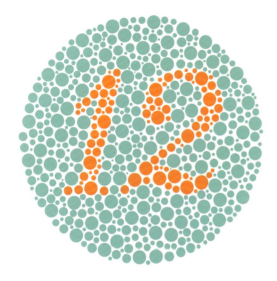

◊ Anyone with either normal or defective color vision will see "12."

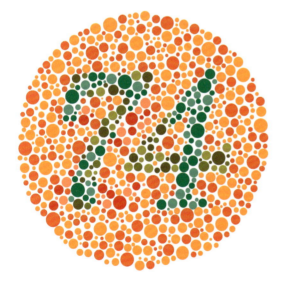

◊ Normal subjects will see "74." Those with red-green deficiencies will see "21."

◊ Normal subjects and those with mild red-green deficiencies will see "42." Those with protanopia and strong protanomalia will see "2" only. Those with deuteranopia and strong deuteranomalia will see "4" only.

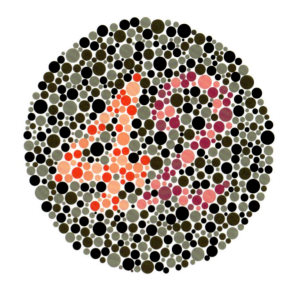

◊ Normal subjects will see "5." Those with red-green deficiencies will see nothing.

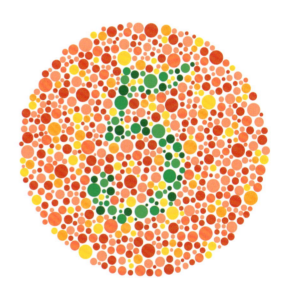

◊ Normal subjects will see "3." Those with red-green deficiencies will see "5."

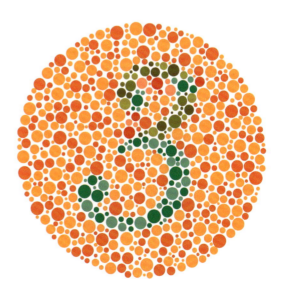

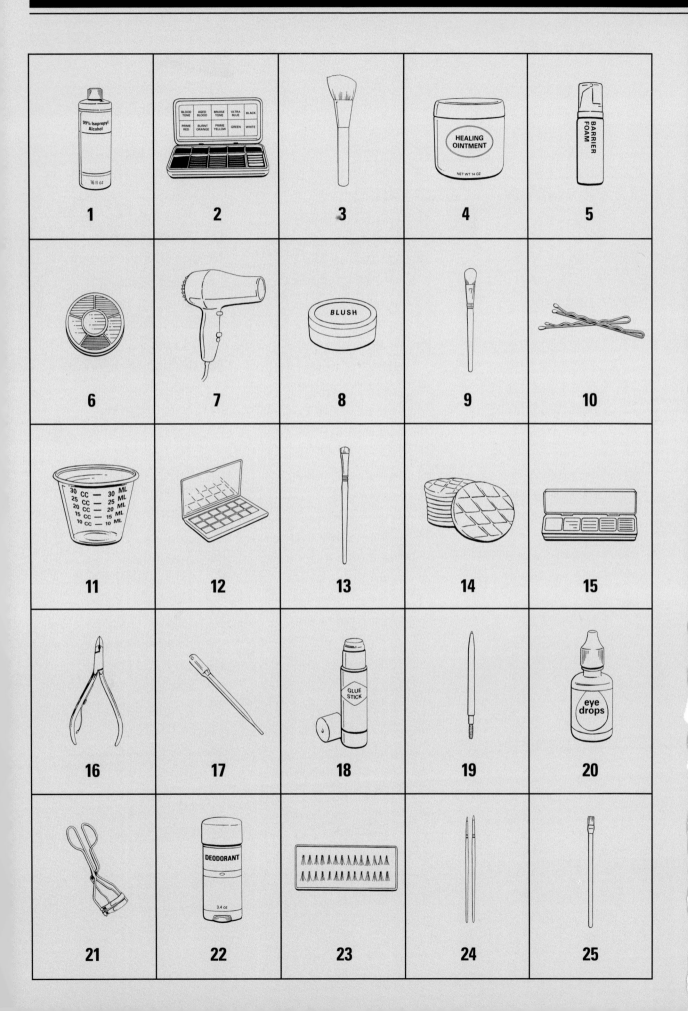

◊ TOOLKIT

1. 99% alcohol
2. Alcohol paint palette
3. Angled powder brush
4. Aquaphor
5. Barrier foam
6. Ben Nye Death Wheel
7. Blow dryer
8. Blush
9. Blush brush
10. Bobby pins
11. CC cup
12. Concealer
13. Concealer brush
14. Cotton rounds
15. Cream paint palette
16. Cuticle cutters
17. Dropper / Pipette
18. Elmer's Purple Glue Stick
19. Eyebrow pencil
20. Eye drops
21. Eyelash curler
22. Face deodorant
23. Fake eyelashes
24. Fine-tip brush
25. Flat eyeliner brush
26. Gaf Quat hair flattener
27. Glue brush
28. Glycerin
29. Half-inch chip brush
30. KY Jelly
31. Large and small foundation brushes
32. Latex-free foam wedge sponges
33. Lip brush
34. Liquid latex
35. Magnifying glass pliers
36. Mascara spoolie
37. Matte lip balm
38. Mattifying primer
39. Medium-hold gel
40. Methyl cellulose
41. Mix holder
42. Moisturizer
43. Non-slanted tweezers and slanted tweezers
44. Old Age Stipples, from least to most extreme:
    Old Age Stipple A
    Old Age Stipple B
    Old Age Stipple C
45. Old Age Stipple Crusty
46. One-inch chip brush
47. PAX paint
48. Powder atomizer / Dispenser
49. Pros-Aide Cream (or Bondo)
50. Pros-Aide Original
51. Puffs fabric rounds, small and large
52. Pure acetone
53. Q-tips, with both round and pointed edges
54. Radiance primer
55. Rattail comb
56. Red stipple sponge
57. Rigid Collodion scarring liquid
58. Round powder brush
59. Round yellow sponge
60. Rubber mask grease paint
61. Setting spray
62. Skin protectant powder
63. Snap hair clips
64. Spatula and metal palette
65. Stomper brush
66. Sunscreen
67. Telesis 8 Adhesive Thinner
68. Telesis 8 Matte Silicone Adhesive
69. Textured orange sponge
70. Tongue depressor
71. Toothbrush
72. Translucent powder
73. Transparent film roll dressing
74. White eyeliner
75. Witch hazel

TOOLKIT

◊ EXTRAS

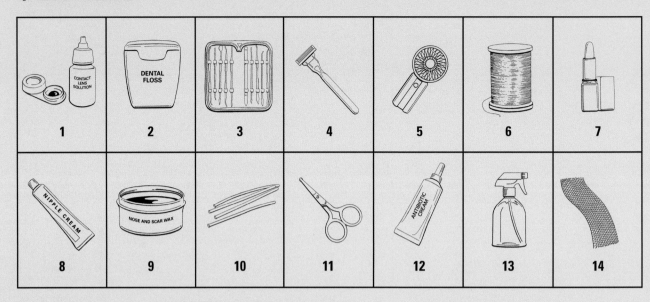

1 Contact lens solution and contact lens cases
Actors will often wear contact lenses on set—proper cleaner and a spare receptacle to keep them in can be useful and sanitary

2 Dental floss
If something breaks and you need to tie it together, this is super strong but also has a little give

3 Dental kit
You will find dental tools useful

4 Gillette razors
For prepping the skin underneath prosthetics

5 Handheld fan
For drying layers in between steps

6 Invisible thread
Good for supporting prosthetics seamlessly

7 Menthol tear stick
Applied under the actor's eyes for crying scenes

8 Nipple cream

9 Nose and scar wax
Also known as Mortician's Wax

10 Party balloons
Used with liquid latex to make blood projectiles (see *How to Make a Neck Bladder*, p. 165)

11 Safety scissors
Best for use on the face, to avoid accidental punctures in a bald cap or otherwise

12 Topical antibiotic cream
To avoid continuity issues that might be caused by a physical Band-Aid, use Neosporin and a transparent liquid bandage

13 Water spray bottle
Useful in a variety of situations—like creating a little extra sweat or to reactive hair products

14 Wig lace
In addition to wig application, this doubles as a method to drag down under eyes and make monster eyes

◊ Kitchen towel (not pictured)
Useful for laying down underneath tools for a sanitary and professional surface, also useful to clean your brushes (see *Skill 7: Cut*, p. 157)

◊ NOTES ON REMOVAL

As an artist, you have a professional responsibility to know your materials—no SPFX makeup is complete without a plan for removal.

1. **244 Fluid**
   Silicone-based remover that also can be used to thin out non-alcohol based airbrush makeup

2. **99% alcohol**
   Required to remove alcohol-based paints

3. **Baby wipes or cleansing cloths**

4. **Barbasol shaving cream**
   When applied on top of skin stained with fake blood, the Barbasol eventually turns pink and lifts the pigment

5. **Facial cleanser and moisturizer**

6. **Bio-Oil**

7. **Hot towel**
   Pack in a zip lock bag with a couple drops of lavender oil. Add some water and microwave in 30 second intervals until steaming. Useful for every removal process, especially for loosening adhesives

8. **Isopropyl myristate**
   Affordable adhesive remover

9. **Nitrile gloves**
   The most chemically resistant kind of glove

10. **Powder puffs**

11. **Removal brushes**

12. **Small bowl**
    To house the remover

13. **Telesis Super Solv**
    More expensive, highly effective adhesive remover

CAST OF CHARACTERS: DEAD & ALIVE

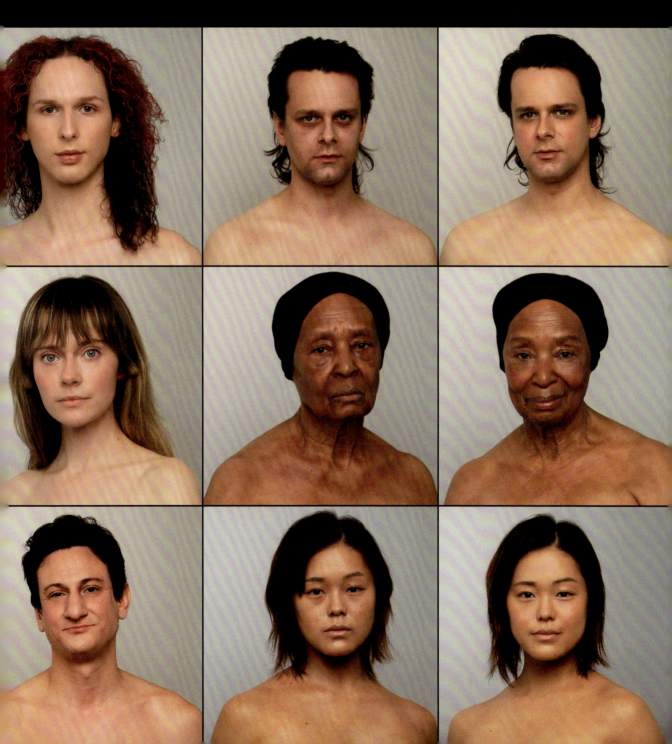

CHAPTER 1a: ALIVE

Skill 1a: Healthy

TOOLS NEEDED	◊ Moisturizer
	◊ Matte lip balm
	◊ Eye drops
	◊ Latex-free foam wedge sponges, including a torn wedge sponge
	◊ Radiance primer
	◊ Mattifying primer
	◊ Concealer
	◊ Foundation brush
	◊ Round powder brush
	◊ Translucent powder
	◊ Stomper brush
	◊ Blush
	◊ Blush brush
	◊ Eyelash curler
	◊ White eyeliner pencil
	◊ Eyebrow pencil
	◊ Q-tips

It is said that in Revolution-era France, severed heads rolled off the guillotine with cheeks in full blush. Was that merely a physiological effect of blood circulation, or were these rolling heads embarrassed to be seen without their bodies? Either way, something uncanny occurred in this bloody moment: the severed heads became beautiful.

Blush is the key component of a classic beauty routine, but its true function is more carnal than most people realize. Blush recaptures the blood that pumps under the skin when temperatures are raised. This lesson concerns color and its relationship to the body more broadly: color correction, highlights, and sculpting the face.

CHAPTER 1

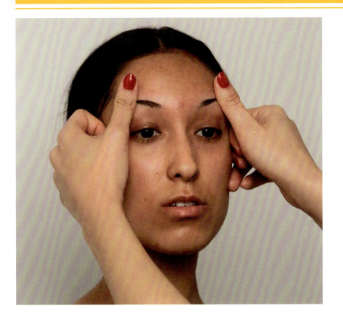

1 Clean and exfoliate the face and lips. Use your fingers to apply your **moisturizer** of choice in a light lymphatic drainage massage (see *Skin Preparation*, p. 12). Apply **matte lip balm** generously. You can also add **eye drops** at this stage, which hydrate and brighten the eyes. Wait one to two minutes, allowing the lips and skin to absorb the product.

2 Lightly run the long side of two **latex-free foam wedge sponges** along the face and lips in a motion similar to the one you use to apply toner. This soaks up excess moisturizer, creating a supple canvas to begin.

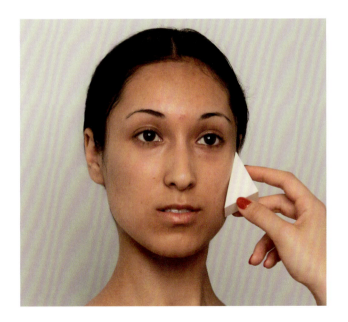

3 Place **radiance primer** on the back of your hand. Using one of the sponges that still has moisturizer on it, apply primer over the orbital bone, at the Cupid's bow, between the eyes, and down the length of the nose. The primer's light-reflective properties will create a subtle glow in these zones.

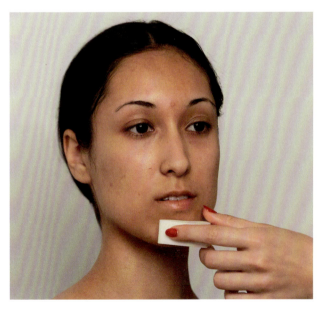

4 Place **mattifying primer** on the back of your hand. Use the second sponge to apply the primer along the T-zone and chin, paying special attention to the sides of the nose. This mattifies the skin where it's shiniest. Use sparingly.

See *How to Cover a Pimple*, p. 41.

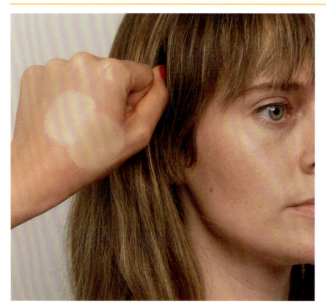

5a Next, select your **concealer**. Place a lighter and darker concealer option on the back of your hand.

5b Create a third color by mixing the two together, keeping the lighter color and the darker color intact on either side—this Venn diagram is crucial. One benefit of mixing makeup on the back of your hand is that it brings it up to body temperature and activates its true color, but you can use a palette here if you are working on multiple subjects.

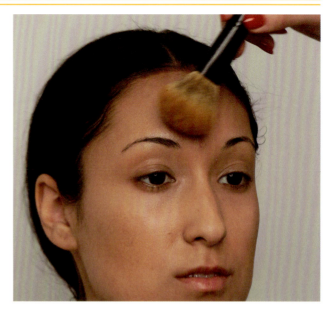

6 Using a **foundation brush**, lightly apply your blended concealer to the center of the face. Since the face is already well moisturized, you will likely not need foundation and the concealer should spread effortlessly over the skin. Brush with a dashing, upwards motion, focusing on redder areas: around the nose, around the mouth, and under the eyes. Make sure to continue your motion down the neck. Note that although the subject might not need coverage, this is how you establish and maintain continuity in their face shade (over the course of shooting a film, for instance). Any areas that you have color corrected, such as a pimple, should be treated like the rest of the face, reassessing if you need more coverage as you go.

At this point, use the color range on the back of your hand to begin sculpting the face lightly with the foundation brush, subtly highlighting with the lighter shade and contouring with the darker. Do this by applying the lighter shade in the same places as the radiance primer, as well as underneath and around the nostrils, and around the corners of the mouth.

Go easy with the darker concealer, tracing along the bottom of the subject's chin and right underneath it. Work it into the cheek hollows, the eyelid creases, and up to the hairline—just a little. You are working around the perimeter of the face and creeping the darker shade inwards toward the middle of the face ever so slightly.

7a Lightly dip the tip of your **round powder brush** into your **translucent powder** and shake off any excess. Gently pat powder in the T-zone, avoiding the under-eye area.

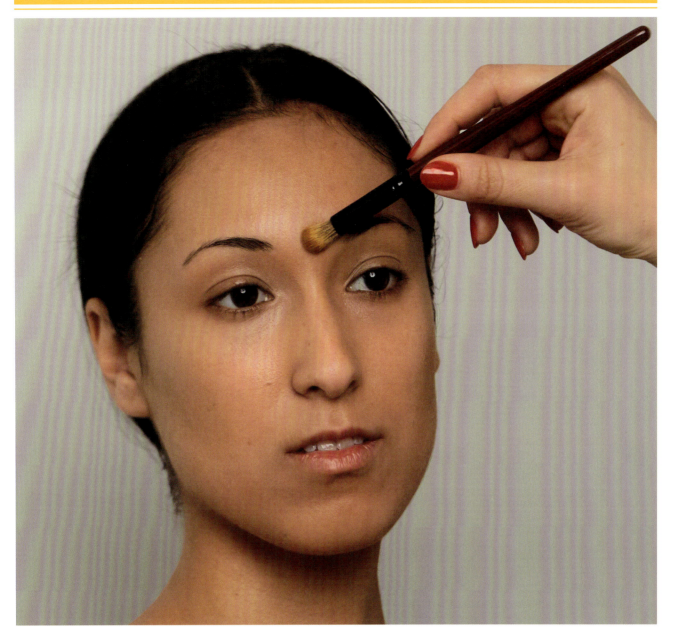

7b Then, use a powdered **stomper brush** over the top of any areas you previously color corrected, to set the layers of pigment.

> Actors look good on camera when their facial features take up more of their face, since that increases the intensity of a given expression. Light concealers heighten your features; the darker concealer frames them.

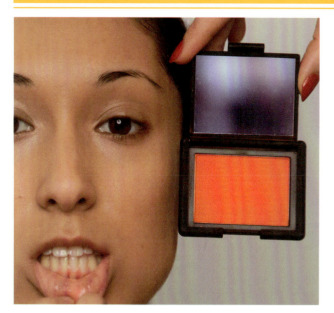

8a To find the best **blush** color, refer to the inside of your subject's mouth. Ask your subject to flip their bottom lip down and assess the full range of color in their mucous membrane. Colors found this way will look natural.

8b Ask your subject to smile, and use a **blush brush** to apply your blush shade to the apples of their cheeks and on the bridge of their nose. Use only what remains on the blush brush over the chin and forehead—you want less intense color on these parts of the face. Blend the blush with the foundation brush that you used in step 7a, p. 36.

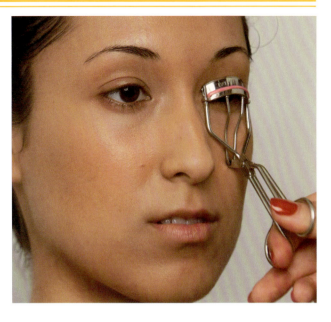

9 For the finishing touches, curl the eyelashes using an **eyelash curler**. If eyelashes are stubborn, you can use a blow dryer to heat up the curler itself—be sure to test it on your hand first so you don't singe the eyelashes.

10 Trace the inner corner of each eye with a **white eyeliner pencil**, making a sideways V. Use your foundation brush to blend it out.

11 Fill in sparse areas of the eyebrows with an **eyebrow pencil** and extend them slightly toward the hairline.

12 Reapply the radiance primer at the high point of the cheekbones and on the brow bone.

13 Apply matte lip balm on the lips with a **Q-tip**.

◊ HOW TO SWEAT

PREP STEP Ask your subject where their sweat points are. These usually include the hairline, nape of neck, nose, upper lip, middle of forehead, and T-zone. However, sweat points vary from person to person.

1 Brush down the hairline with a **mascara spoolie** dipped in **glycerin**. Use your fingers to dab the glycerin all around the temples, the back of the neck, and wherever else your subject may naturally sweat.

2 To create beaded sweat, spray the desired area with water.

◊ HOW TO COVER A PIMPLE

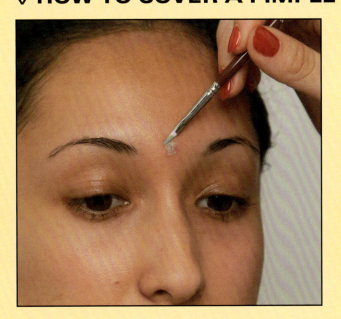

To cover a pimple (or a hickey), you will need to use color theory (see *Color Theory*, p. 17).

1 Taking a **fine-tip brush** and your **cream makeup palette**, apply a very small amount of green cream right on top of the pimple. (The depth of the green cream should be determined by the lightness or darkness of the concealer you have matched to your subject already.) Make sure not to place any on the healthy surrounding skin—it's not necessary.

Then apply **translucent powder** with a **stomper brush** over the top.

Remember, pimples should always be well moisturized to prevent flaking. Skin needs to breathe, and too much product only calls more attention to a blemish.

If continuity isn't an issue for a film, it can sometimes be more interesting for the character to leave a pimple uncovered. It can make the rest of the makeup more convincing.

◊ HOW TO APPLY A TATTOO

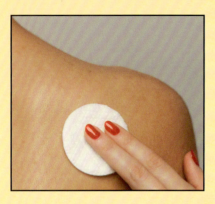

1 Clean the skin by applying **witch hazel** with a **cotton round**.

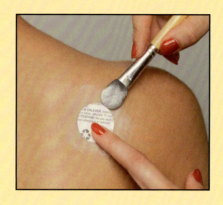

2 Cut out your choice of **temporary tattoo**, leaving the plastic film intact. Place the temporary tattoo on the skin, face down. Lightly powder around it with **loose translucent powder**. This will denote the placement.

When purchasing and drawing tattoos, look for navy instead of black. This will better mimic the appearance of a real tattoo.

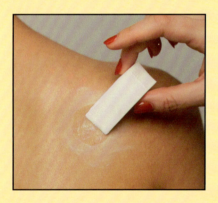

3 With your **latex-free foam wedge sponge**, stipple a thin layer of **Pros-Aide** inside the outline you've created. This will help the tattoo adhere longer.

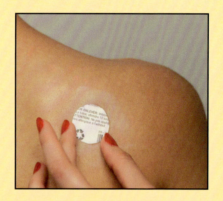

4 Once the Pros-Aide has completely dried to clear, peel off the plastic backing and adhere the tattoo to the designated area.

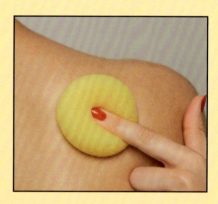

5 Take a damp sponge and press down on the tattoo (we use a **round yellow sponge**, like the Ben Nye Hydra Sponge, due to its water retention, but you can also use a paper towel or cloth).

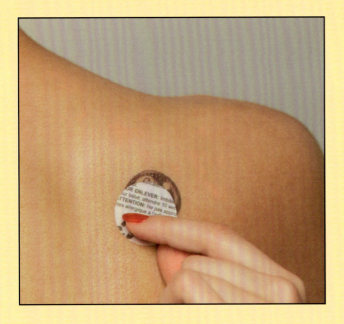

6   If the application is properly executed, the paper should slide off with ease.

7   Allow the tattoo to dry and apply another light layer of Pros-Aide on top with your wedge sponge. Now the tattoo is completely encapsulated in Pros-Aide and will not come off.

8   Blend the edges of the tattoo with **99% alcohol** using a **Q-tip**. Brush and set lightly with powder to remove tackiness.

9   Finally, if excess powder is giving away the tattoo's edges, you can clean it off with water. The key to making a temporary tattoo look realistic is to keep a little powder or light foundation on top to mimic the dead skin that usually collects on tattoos.

SKILL 1a

◊ **HOW TO "REMOVE" A TATTOO**

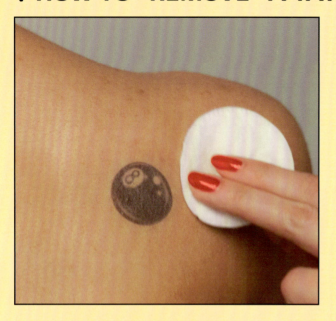

1 In film and photography, you will have to ensure tattoos are copyright cleared. It is illegal to use a tattoo artist's work without properly crediting them—which is where this skill can come into play. First clean the area with **99% alcohol**.

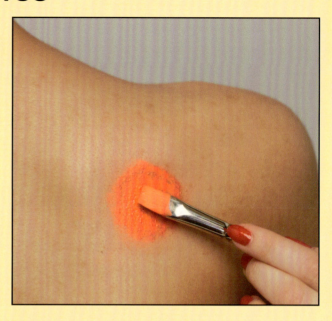

2 Identify your **alcohol paint** in the corresponding blue color-correction shade: salmon for lighter skin tones and orange for deeper skin tones (see *Color Theory*, p. 17). Paint your tattoo in layers, allowing it to dry in between, until it is fully covered. Let dry fully before moving onto the next step.

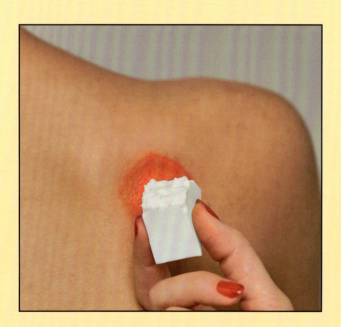

3 Pick at one side of a wedge sponge to create a coarser texture—this **torn wedge sponge** will reappear in many future skills.

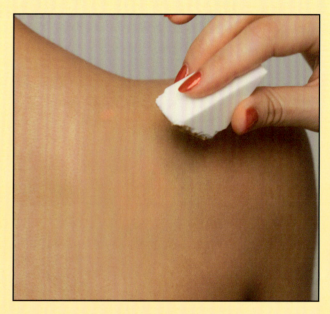

4 Using your torn wedge sponge, apply **PAX paint** over the tattoo, matching it to the subject's skin color. As mentioned, building layers is all about product interactions. Be mindful of your base paint material and make sure not to put something on top that would melt it. Dust with loose **translucent powder** to set.

CHAPTER 1   45

◊ HOW TO CRY WITH MASCARA

1   Apply **mascara** with your **spoolie**, using as much product as possible. Make sure to move from right to left across the lash line, taking advantage of every axis. Use the tip of the wand where the product tends to build up.

2   Wet your spoolie with water and rub your subject's lashes from side to side while their eyes are shut.

This skill works best with traditional mascara. For more staying power and drama, first apply a layer of waterproof mascara, but note that this skill will not work with waterproof mascara alone.

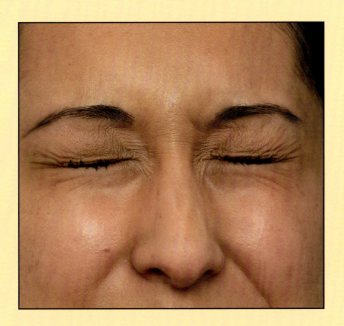

3   Ask them to blink harder than usual to create natural pooling in the contours of the orbital bone.

4   With the subject's eyes open, take a **fine-tip brush** and exaggerate the shapes in the makeup according to your style. Use additional mascara as paint if needed, keeping in mind that the less brushwork, the better. Rub the "tears" with your clean fingers to create a more smudged effect (you can also ask the subject to rub their eyes). As long as you don't over-paint, anything goes.

ALIVE

NAME	Sam
AGE	20
OCCUPATION	Ballet dancer
HOMETOWN	New Paltz, NY

White eyeliner helps Sam's eyes look as awake—and alive—as possible. We add additional white eyeliner down the center of the eyelid, right below the waterline, and in the inner and outer corners of the eye. These white marks are then blended with an **angled shadow brush**.

Sam's lashes are coated in a light dusting of **translucent powder** for volume, followed by several swipes of a **mascara spoolie dipped in black eyeliner** (of course, you can also use **mascara**). Run a clean **mascara spoolie** through to remove any excess clumps.

Apply **fake eyelashes** by dipping the knot in **eyelash glue**. After allowing the glue to fully dry and become tacky, apply individual lashes along the outer edge of the limbus on both the top and bottom lash line, plus one at the outer corner of the top lash line to elongate the eye shape.

Try this optical illusion from Allan Snyder, Marilyn Monroe's makeup artist: smudge a **contour shade** just beneath the outer corner of the eye in order to mimic the shadow cast by heavy upper lashes.

Use your fingers to tap **Aquaphor** at the high points of the face where the light will hit: the cheekbones, brow bones, the space between the eyes, the Cupid's bow, eyelids, lips, and collarbones.

ADDITIONAL TOOLS	◊ White eyeliner (liquid as well as kohl)
	◊ Angled shadow brush
	◊ Translucent powder
	◊ Mascara spoolie dipped in black eyeliner (or mascara)
	◊ Mascara spoolie
	◊ Fake eyelashes
	◊ Eyelash glue
	◊ Cream paint palette in contour tones
	◊ Aquaphor

CHAPTER 1b: DEAD

Skill 1b: Ill

TOOLS NEEDED	◊ Moisturizer
	◊ Mattifying primer
	◊ Cream paint palette
	◊ Foundation brush

You can portray a character's emotional state or declining health over the course of a film by adjusting their makeup. In the case of downfall, for example, a character may develop a sallow look. A broken heart shows in the face.

Illness makeup can be used as a subtle narrative device, but it can also be an opportunity for exaggeration. It involves manipulating the planes of the face by sinking and raising features. It's actually a kind of contour makeup, and in that sense, stage makeup, too—a method of playing to the back of the room.

CHAPTER 1

55

PREP STEP   Apply **moisturizer** to make a slick surface for the cream makeup you're about to apply (see *Skin Preparation: Massage Technique*, p, 14). Make sure to omit the lip exfoliation and balm. You want the lips to be as scaly as possible.

1   Using your hands or a makeup sponge, apply **mattifying primer** all over the face. This will remove any dewiness—or "life"—in the face.

 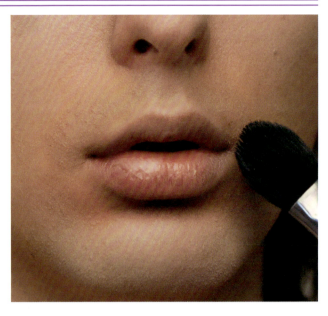

2 Find a pallid color on your **cream paint palette** (we like Ben Nye's Death Wheel). Use the side of your hand as your mixing surface and apply with a **foundation brush** to your subject's cheeks, forehead, Cupid's bow, chin, and under the neck. The goal here is to make the features protrude—much like the white zones in traditional skull makeup (see *Figure 1*).

3 Still using the foundation brush, work the same shade into the lips, grazing over them and focusing on the center: the dryer the lips, the better.

Figure 1

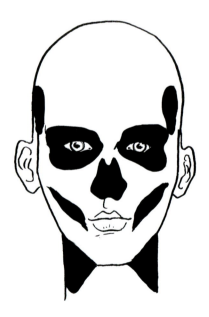 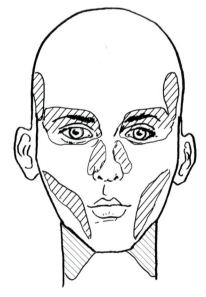

Skull　　　　　　　　　　Contour

4 Using the dark red-brown from the same palette and the foundation brush, follow the crescent shape of the orbital bone with a back-and-forth motion. Repeat this movement lightly a few times. (By brushing more tentatively, you will feel where the bones are telling you to stop, ultimately giving the makeup a more natural appearance.)

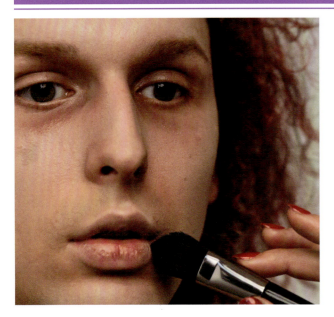 

5 Continue moving around the face with this shade, brushing under and around the nose, and down the nasolabial folds to the corners of the mouth and the immediate surrounding area.

6 Again, using the skull as your guide, work the cream paint down the cheekbones, under the jaw, and down the center of the trachea. Everywhere you see a shadow, sink it, follow it. When it comes to sickly makeup, it's important to always blend your contours in downward strokes rather than up.

7 Blend all the paint at the hairline, alternating between the two tones.

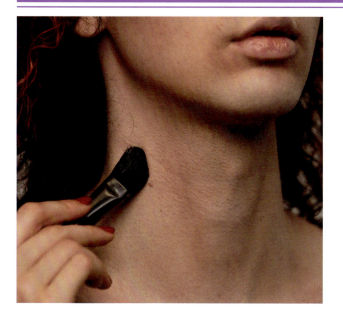 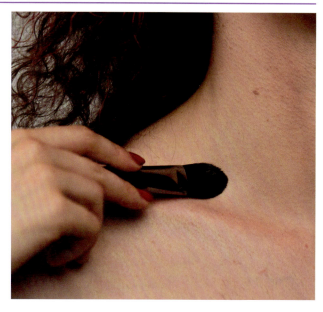

8   Brush the lighter color onto the trachea, as well as down the sides of the neck. Follow by brushing the darker shade in a V shape leading down to the clavicle.

9   Trace along the length of the clavicle with the lighter shade, followed by the darker. You can create a circle in the middle of the collarbone where the two tones meet.

DEAD

NAME	Nat
AGE	25
OCCUPATION	Makeup Artist
HOMETOWN	Minneapolis, MN

For Nat, we use beauty makeup methods with special effects materials. For our color palette, we use **Ben Nye's Death Wheel**, which offers a selection of colors that special effects artists use to take the life out of someone's face.

First we deposit these pigments on Nat's face with a contour makeup structure. Then, instead of blending in downward strokes as is typical for this illness makeup palette (see *Skill 1b: Ill*, p. 53), we blend our contours upwards in the beauty contour tradition for a dramatically morbid look.

Next we smudge **pinkish red lip liner** around the eyes to enhance her pallor and to bring out her waterlines. You can also use the mucous membrane as a site to create the look of irritation.

We dust a **green iridescent powder** onto the high points of her face to fight the purple tone of the background. The use of unharmonious colors contributes to the overall deadly look.

ADDITIONAL TOOLS	◊ Ben Nye Death Wheel
	◊ Pinkish red lip liner
	◊ Green iridescent powder

CHAPTER 2: OLD

Skill 2: Old Age Stipple

TOOLS NEEDED	◊ Witch hazel
	◊ Cotton round
	◊ Barrier foam
	◊ Latex-free foam wedge sponges, including a torn wedge sponge
	◊ Old Age Stipple C (this stipple creates a heavy wrinkling effect; lighter versions are available in A, B, and the heaviest version, Crusty)
	◊ Blow dryer
	◊ Translucent powder
	◊ Round powder brush

Sun hits truck drivers from the left. As a result, they wrinkle more on that side. Smokers, who pucker their mouths around a cigarette, age with vertical lines around the mouth. A more descriptive term for wrinkles might be expression lines—they're the face revealing, in old age, the dominant patterns of a lifetime.

Creating the appearance of old age demands study. First, the makeup artist must imagine the arc of a character's life to understand what aging looks like for them. Second, the makeup artist must find out what expression lines their subject already has. We locate these lines and deepen them—you cannot find a wrinkle that was not there to begin with unless you use prosthetics (typically silicone, see *Skill 6: Prosthetic Application*, p. 141).

Stretch, stipple, powder: this is a three-part lesson in aging subjects on the face, neck, and hands, or simply creating a coarser and rougher skin texture for use under monster makeup.

1 Apply **witch hazel** with a **cotton round** across the forehead, down the nose, and down the neck. If you have a subject with sensitive skin, you can add a layer of **barrier foam** using your **latex-free foam wedge sponges**. Creating this barrier will also encourage the stipple to lift with less effort at the removal stage.

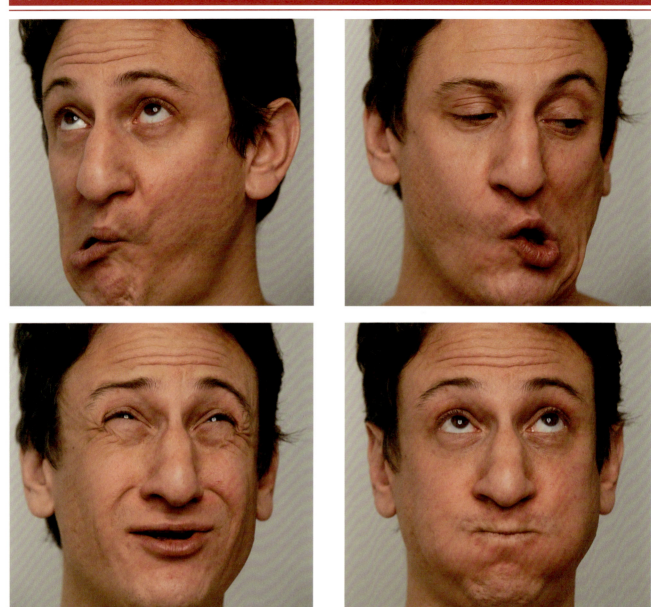

2a Ask your subject to exaggerate their facial expressions so you can find their natural creases.

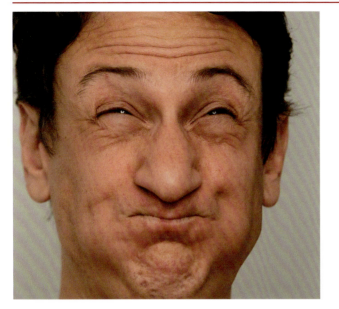
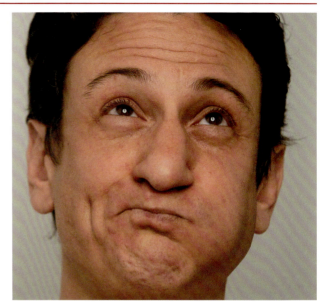
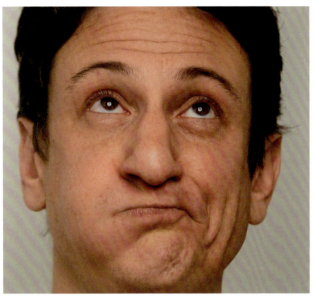

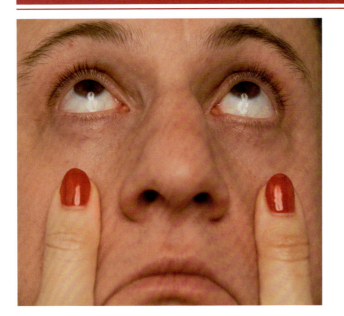

2b Pull the skin on either side of the targeted crease until it is smooth. By stretching and stippling the skin in the zones and directions shown here, you will create wrinkles in the most realistic places.

> When stretching and applying stipple around the eye area, make sure your subject shuts their eyelids so they don't get any of the product in their eyes.

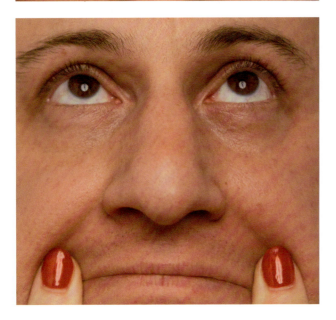

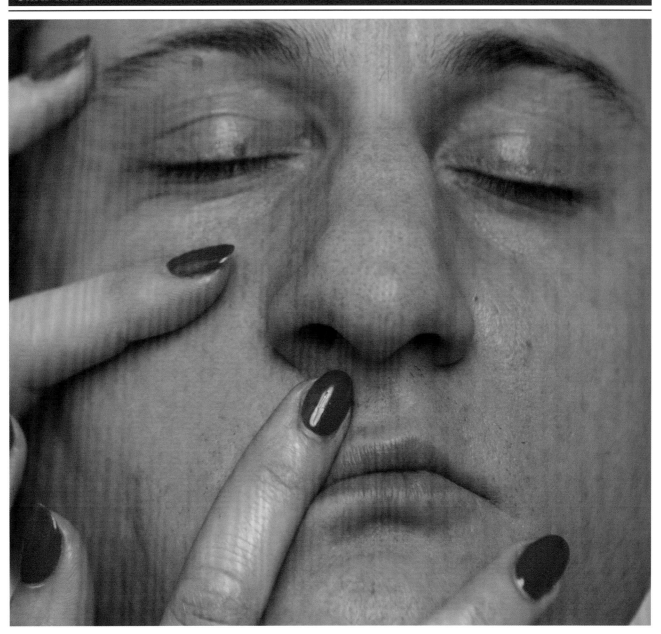

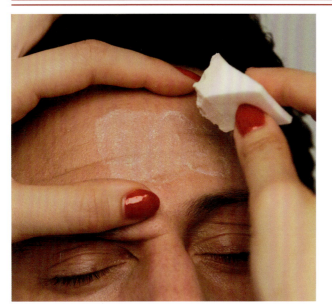

3 For the following steps, we applied the stipple at three key "aging" areas: the forehead, the crow's feet, and the nasolabial folds. Take a latex-free foam wedge sponge and rip it in half. Using your fingers, pick one half apart at the torn side to make an even rougher texture for stippling (see *How to "Remove" a Tattoo*, p. 44). Dip this **torn wedge sponge** into your **Old Age Stipple C** and apply one thin layer to your chosen area, holding the skin taut with two fingers as you work. Make sure to let the first layer dry before you add another—you can speed up this process with a **blow dryer** on the cool setting.

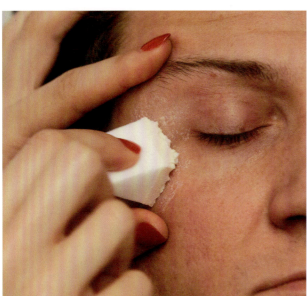

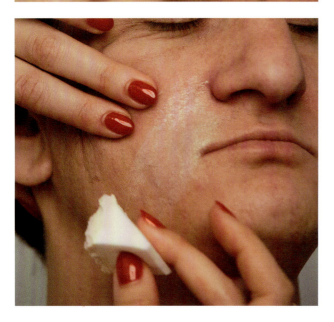

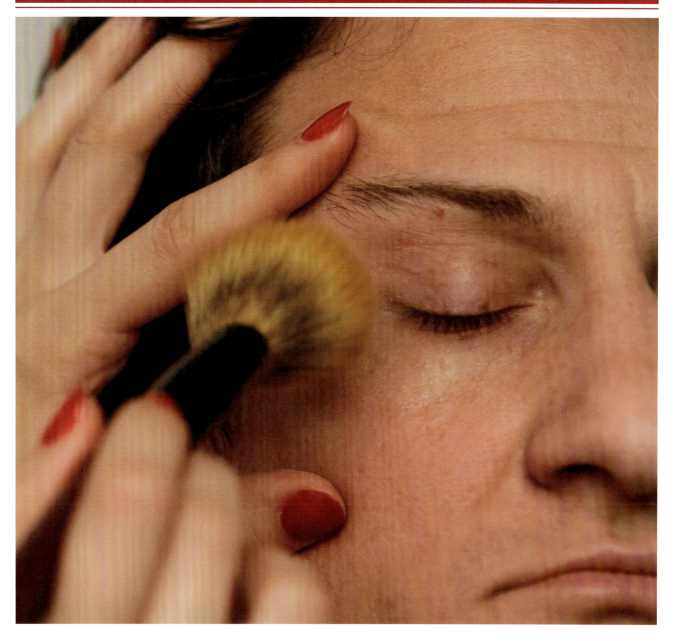

4 Finally, brush **translucent powder** over the stipple with a **round powder brush**, keeping the skin stretched with your fingers. Once you're done, you can release the skin and the section should wrinkle realistically.

76 SKILL 2

◊ **HOW TO AGE HAIR**

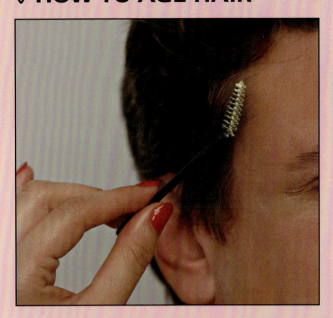 

To apply gray streaks to clean hair, apply **rubber mask grease paint** to the hair using a **45-degree-angled mascara spoolie**. (To get the appropriate shade, you can mix white and yellow for more of a gray-white.) Brush the paint down and then backcomb upwards to coat the hair, following any natural graying patterns that may be present. Optional: set with hairspray.

◊ **HOW TO "REMOVE" A TOOTH**

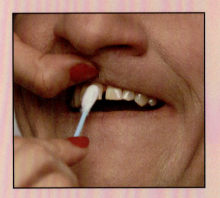  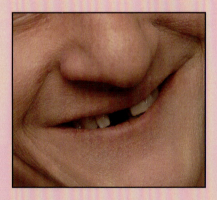

To paint a tooth, first clean it with **99% alcohol** so the paint can adhere properly. Then, using a **fine-tip brush**, paint the tooth with your chosen shade of **alcohol paint**.

This technique can also be used to create a tooth gap or to indicate decay.

CHAPTER 2

◊ HOW TO AGE NAILS

To create nicotine-stained nails, follow the steps for *How to "Remove" a Tooth* on the surface of the nail. In this case, however, add more **99% alcohol** to the alcohol paint and mix it on the lid of the palette to create more of a wash. This technique can be used on teeth as well if your character is a smoker. The color we use here is appropriately called Nicotine.

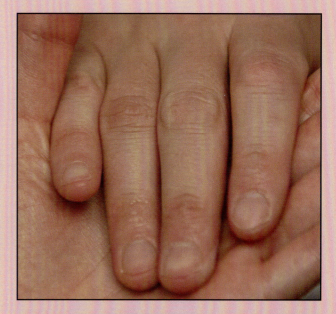

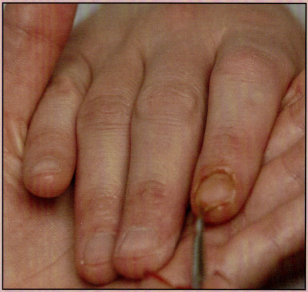

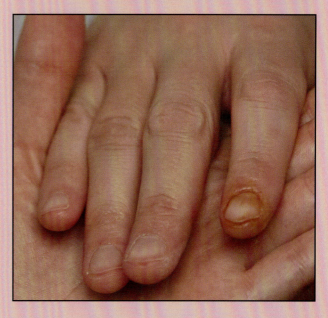

Since carrying around a full set of nail polishes is cumbersome, and since nail polish takes time to dry, it's often more convenient to color the nail with alcohol paint and then apply a single clear top coat of nail polish for shine and durability.

OLD

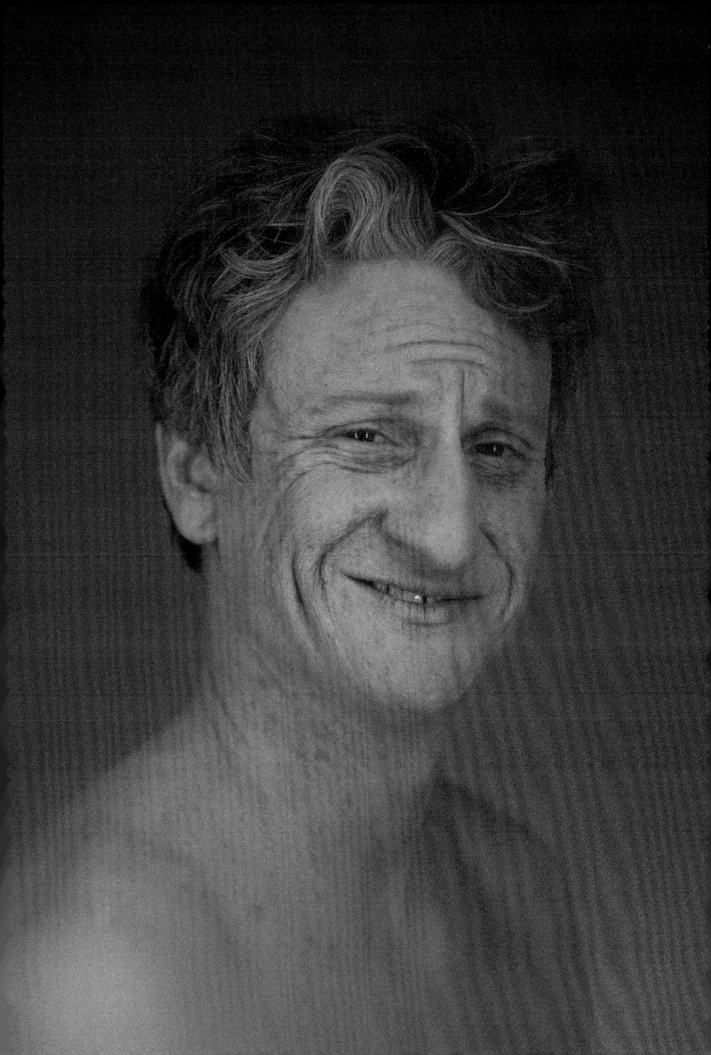

NAME	Stephen
AGE	39
OCCUPATION	Filmmaker
HOMETOWN	Minneapolis, MN

Convincing old-age makeup must show the signs of thinning skin. To begin, we draw in what lies underneath: veins. To select the right color tone, look at the inside of your subject's elbows. If their veins are greener, it means they have a warmer skin tone; if the veins are more blue, a cooler skin tone. Noodling with a **fine-tip brush**, we form veins around Steven's temples, neck, and eyes.

There's a similar ethos behind exposed capillaries. Use a fine-tip brush with a corresponding **"capillary" color corrector** around the jowls, at the nasolabial folds, and around the nostrils.

When using the alcohol paints, add 1–3 drops of **99% alcohol** into each cell to activate the color. Remember: if you allow the alcohol to soak into the color for several seconds, you will get a more opaque tint.

Freckles are nearly as important as wrinkles for realistically aged skin that has been exposed to the sun over the years. Stephen's age spots are achieved using brown shades of **alcohol paints** that are dotted all over: the darker the tone, the more intense the freckle. You can also take a technique from beauty makeup and use an **eyebrow pencil** instead. Try alternating between a blonde and brunette pencil, using a light bouncing motion to apply.

To make Stephen's under-eye bags, we use a **glazing gel** by Skin Illustrator. These are transparent water-based colors that also come in handy for bruise and injury work. The Character 2 tone, a kind of brown-bruise shade, is applied with a **one-inch chip brush** under the eyes to create realistically tired eye bags.

ADDITIONAL TOOLS
- Fine-tip brush
- Salmon/orange color corrector
- 99% alcohol
- Alcohol paint palette in skin tones
- Eyebrow pencil
- Glazing gel
- One-inch chip brush

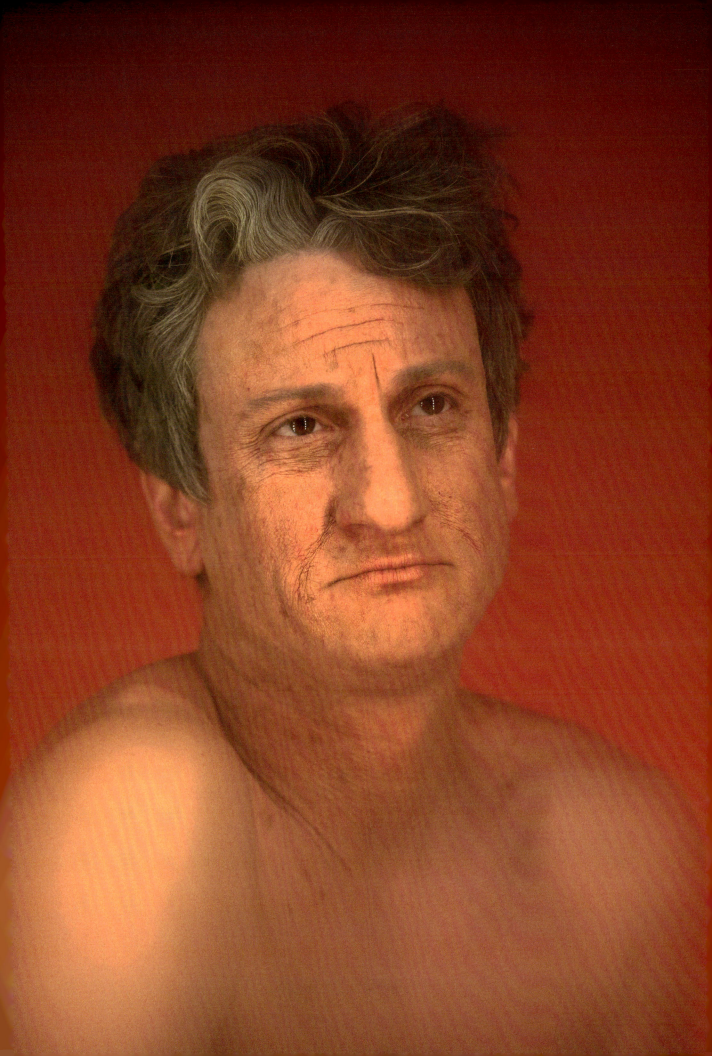

CHAPTER 3: YOUNG

CHAPTER 3

Skill 3: Skin Manipulation

TOOLS NEEDED	◊ Cotton round
	◊ Witch hazel
	◊ Face tape

Beauty and youth are often conflated, but as a makeup artist you must see them distinctly. Face tape is marketed as a beauty product, but it is also a versatile tool for character design.

This lesson, which centers around a tape kit, can be used to make your subject look like a younger version of themselves for a flashback scene, or to expose the whites of their eyes for a more complex horror makeup. Apply tapes unevenly to mimic a stroke.

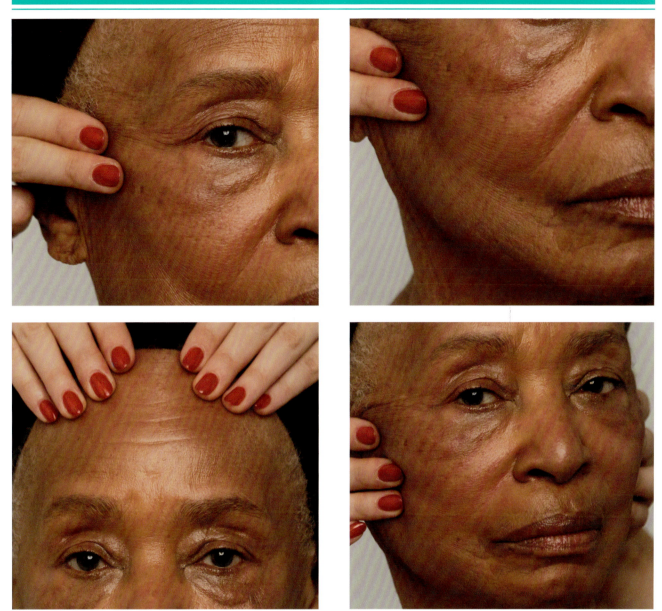

1 Place your fingers on the face to feel where skin pulling will be most impactful: you can gently lift the skin to see where wrinkles may be effectively smoothed out. On our subject, these are the most effective places.

2 Using a **cotton round**, apply **witch hazel** onto the face where the tape will be placed, about an inch inwards from the hairline. Repeat this on the opposite side of the face, ensuring that the placement is symmetrical.

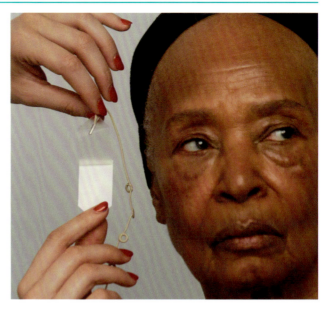

3 Peel off the paper backing of your chosen **face tape**.

> One of the most useful characteristics of this tool is that if your subject needs a break—for instance, you're working with an actor on a long shoot—you can unhook the loops.

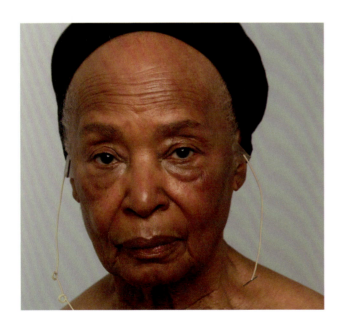

4 Apply the tape. You will need to alternate between facing your subject and looking in the mirror to make sure the tape is applied evenly on either side.

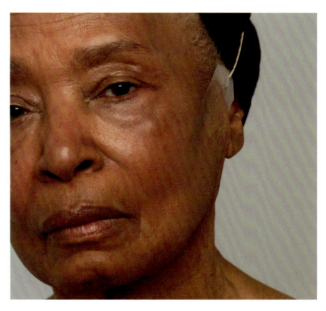

5 Now begin the pull. There's a toggle on one side of the straps and loops on the other. Standing behind your subject, pull back the skin using both straps and place the toggle inside one of the loops when you have reached an appropriate level of stretch. Note that if your subject has hair, you will need to hide the elastic according to the hairstyle.

CHAPTER 3

◇ HOW TO REVERSE COUNTOUR

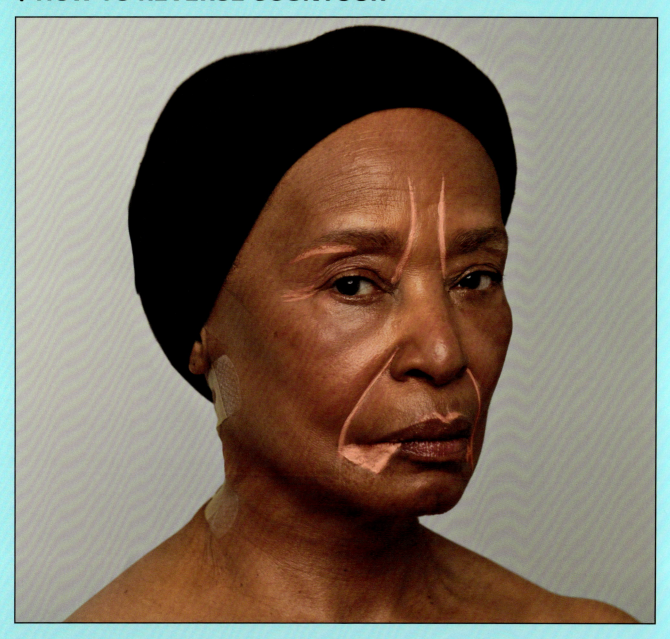

Look at your subject's face and identify where there is volume loss (areas where features tend to sink in with age, such as the nasolabial folds). With your **fine-tip brush** and a **cream paint palette**, trace along the lines of the areas you've identified. You'll need to do this in the shade that suits the subject's skin: white for lighter skin tones, light pink for medium skin tones, salmon for darker skin tones, and orange for deep skin tones.

YOUNG

NAME	Dr. Theda
AGE	82
OCCUPATION	Club owner, author
HOMETOWN	St. Louis, MO

Aged or damaged skin needs moisture, so avoid heavy foundations and powders when possible. Keep **eye drops** handy, too (as you age, your eyes become drier).

It's important to make sure that all products, from shadows to blushes, are blended well. For reverse contouring (see *How to Reverse Contour*, p. 91), a **foundation brush** is used to really blend those lines into Theda's skin.

For the beauty component of Theda's look, we use an **iridescent purple eyeshadow** as a "wash" over the eyelids from the inner to the outer corners, and a **medium-brown lipstick with a satin finish** on her lips. Finally, the same iridescent purple eyeshadow is applied to the center of her lips.

ADDITIONAL TOOLS	◊ Eye drops
	◊ Foundation brush
	◊ Foundation
	◊ Iridescent purple eyeshadow
	◊ Medium-brown lipstick with a satin finish

CHAPTER 4: BALD

Skill 4: Bald Cap

TOOLS NEEDED	◊ Bald cap (we use Kryolan)
	◊ Water spray bottle
	◊ Medium-hold gel
	◊ Rattail comb
	◊ Snap hair clips
	◊ Witch hazel
	◊ Unscented roll-on antiperspirant (we use Stop The Sweat)
	◊ Latex-free foam wedge sponges, including two torn wedge sponges
	◊ Pros-Aide
	◊ 99% alcohol
	◊ Safety scissors
	◊ Cotton batting, cotton balls, or cotton rounds
	◊ Acetone
	◊ Pointed Q-tip
	◊ PAX paint
	◊ Translucent powder
	◊ Round powder brush or powder puff
	◊ Foundation brush
	◊ Foundation
	◊ Setting spray

People often account for what is mysterious about the Mona Lisa by talking about her smile. But let's focus on the absence of her eyebrows to understand what makes her expression inscrutable.

Giving someone new eyebrows, or removing their eyebrows altogether, has the power to transform their range of expression. To do that, you must create baldness—one of the essential skills of makeup and special effects.

Bald caps can be used simply to make someone bald, but they also have many other functions. They are required to make a three-dimensional copy of the face—a process known as lifecasting—which is necessary to build custom prosthetics. They are needed for applying a hairpiece, reshaping a hairline, and attaching devil horns. They create a blank canvas.

When buying bald caps (see *Suppliers*, p. 178), be mindful of the size of your subject's head and the amount of hair they have, which will determine the correct size of their bald cap.

PREP STEP For a film, if you're not going to see the back of your subject's head on screen or if it will be hidden (with a collar, turtleneck, or scarf, for example), you can simply slick the hair down the nape of the neck before you apply the **bald cap**. Otherwise, proceed with hair wrapping. Begin by dampening the hair with a **water spray bottle** (use room-temperature water—cold water can be jarring).

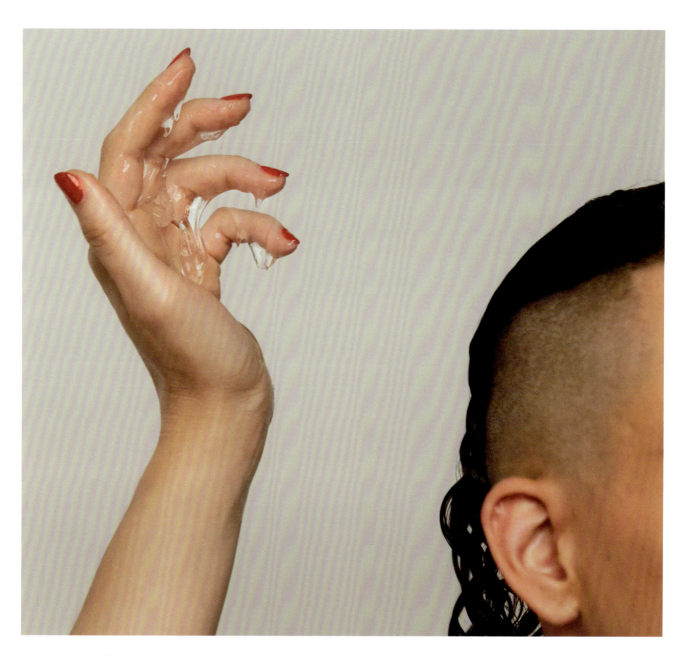

1 After brushing the hair evenly, apply **medium-hold gel** throughout. You want a texture that is workable but not crispy.

2 Using a **rattail comb**, take a half-inch- to an inch-long section of hair along the hairline between your fingers and place it forward, out of the way. You will come back to it later.

3 Divide the remaining hair into two sections and criss-cross one section over the other, maintaining as much smoothness as possible.

> There are many ways to wrap hair. Different hairstyles, shapes, and textures call for different techniques, and you must remain flexible.

4 Using **snap hair clips**, fasten the hair at the point where you have crossed the sections. You should secure and finesse using clips as needed. (We prefer snap clips because they follow the contour of the head and will not poke up and rip through your bald cap.)

5 Return to the front-lying piece of hair from step 2 and lay it straight against your previously wrapped hair. This is how you ensure that the bald cap lies as flat and as realistically as possible against the hairline.

6   Clean the skin with **witch hazel** where the edge of the bald cap is going to sit. At this stage, you can apply a face deodorant to prevent perspiration from forming underneath the bald cap and loosening the bond of the adhesive. Many artists use a brand called Stop The Sweat, but you can use any **unscented roll-on antiperspirant**. (It's all aluminum in the end, so make sure your subject is okay with that ingredient.)

7   For the initial placement of the bald cap, apply glue only to the forehead. Use a **latex-free foam wedge sponge** to apply **Pros-Aide** somewhere between the hairline and the eyebrows, making sure not to get it on either. Pros-Aide and hair do not mix well, so you should always create a barrier of hair gel (you could also use Telesis 8 Matte Silicone Adhesive or Gaf Quat).

8   Wipe the bald cap down on both sides with **99% alcohol**, noting where the front is (this is typically indicated with a sticker or a pen marking provided by the manufacturer).

9   Fold the bottom of the bald cap up, one quarter at a time, as you place it over your subject's head. The trick here is to land evenly on the forehead, as this is the part of the bald cap that will be most visible on camera. Next, carefully pull it three quarters of the way over the head.

10 Use your fingers to press the bald cap down on the forehead to further adhere the glue and make sure there is a secure attachment.

11 Using **safety scissors**, cut the bald cap from the cheeks upwards, toward your subject's eyes. Do this on one side and then the other, and finish by cutting between both sides above the eyes. Don't cut too close to where you want the bald cap to sit—be sure to leave some flashing.

12 If you need to alter the shape of your subject's head, use **cotton batting**, **cotton balls**, or even **cotton rounds**. Place a small piece where there's any dip or unevenness in the topography of the head, then place a larger piece on top of that as needed. You should be able to work this into the existing hair wrap to secure it. At the very least, the cotton batting will even out the surface and conceal the clips used so far. It can also be a great opportunity for design, from creating a conehead shape to mimicking subdermal implants.

13 Use a latex-free foam wedge sponge to apply Pros-Aide to the nape of the neck, where the bald cap will end. Cover the skin everywhere there's no hair, including the backs of the ears. As you can see on our subject's head, there's a wide surface area to stick the bald cap on. Let dry until clear.

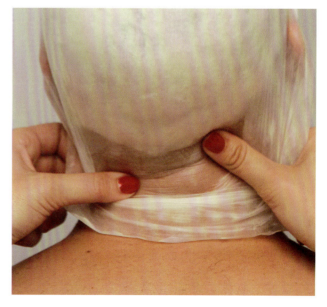

14 Ask your subject to tilt their head back. Pull the back of the bald cap over the head, and press it down at the nape of the neck, keeping it taut. Watch your nails to avoid splitting the bald cap.

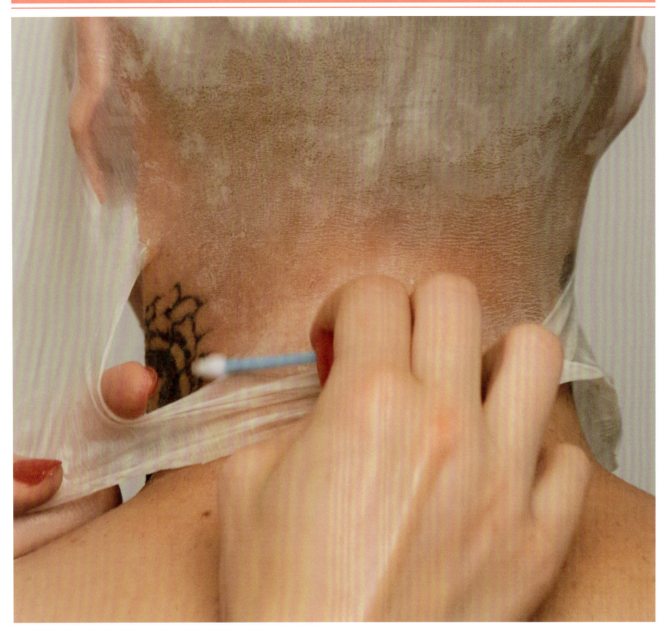

15 Once the bald cap has completely adhered, firmly apply **acetone** to the outside edge of the bald cap with a **pointed Q-tip**, all the way around the head. This process of melting the edge where the glue ends and the flashing begins is typically referred to as "burning off the flashing."

16 To release the subject's ears, use your safety scissors to cut around the ear, burn off flashing in the surrounding area, and then "pop" the ear out. Repeat this step for the other ear.

17 With your **torn wedge sponge**, apply a layer of Pros-Aide all over the surface and around the edges of the bald cap (see S*kill 6: Prosthetic Application*, p. 141, for another use of this technique). This process encapsulates the bald cap in a uniform material and provides the right skin-like texture in anticipation of the **PAX paint** layer you will apply next.

18 Using a clean torn wedge sponge, spread PAX paint over the entire surface of the bald cap in your muscle layer shade (see *Skill 6: Prosthetic Application*, p. 141, for more on the muscle layer shade).

> You always need to allow Pros-Aide to fully dry before applying another compound on top. You can let it dry naturally or speed things up with a blow dryer. If you trap it under a surface before it has completely dried, it will look white, interfering with your paint job, and will not stick properly, if at all.

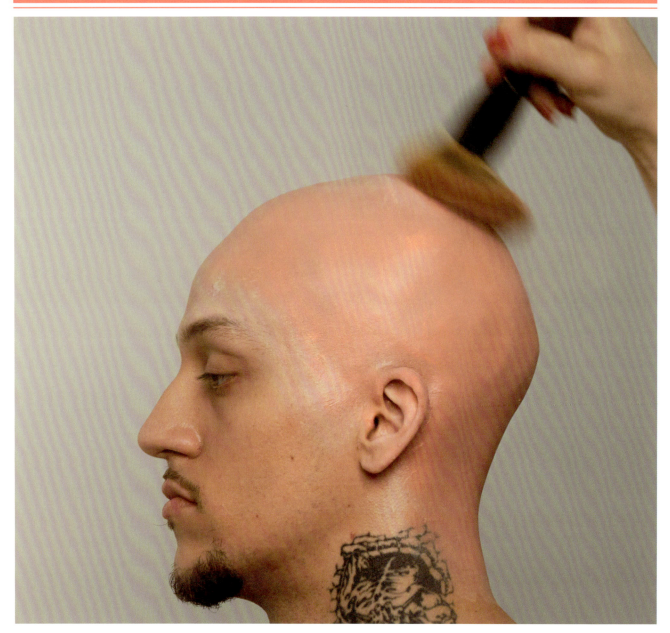

19 Evenly apply **translucent powder** to the head using a technique we call the "Schubert sprinkle and tap": sprinkle powder in an even layer over the desired area, then buff it out with what remains on the **round powder brush** or **powder puff**.

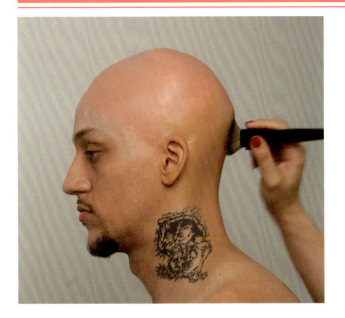

20 Using a **foundation brush**, brush **foundation** over the muscle layer. To blend the bald cap fully, don't forget to extend the foundation onto the subject's cheeks, chin, neck, forehead, and nose.

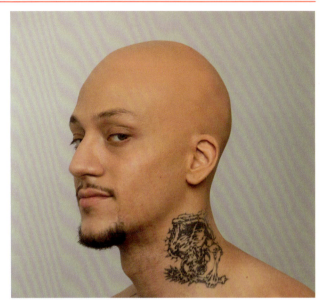

21 After another light dusting of powder (remember to extend down onto the face), mist the entire head with **setting spray**.

> Keep the surface of the bald cap dewy by coating your hands in KY Jelly and pressing them on the top.

◊ HOW TO COVER EYEBROWS

1 Clean the eyebrows with **witch hazel**. Then, with a clean **mascara spoolie**, backcomb the eyebrows, brushing upwards in the opposite direction of their natural angle of growth.

2 Apply **Elmer's Purple Glue Stick** to the eyebrow areas, first brushing it back in the same direction you spoolied, and then rubbing it in every direction. Don't be afraid to truly coat every hair.

3 Use your spoolie to brush all the hairs up, this time following your subject's natural angle of growth.

4 Apply more glue in layers. Wait for it to dry in between coats. When the purple turns clear, it's time for another coat.

5 Use a **metal spatula** to hold down the top of the eyebrows and finesse and smooth out the glue.

6 With a **powder puff**, apply **translucent powder** to the brow. This smooths and fills in any gaps and prepares it for painting.

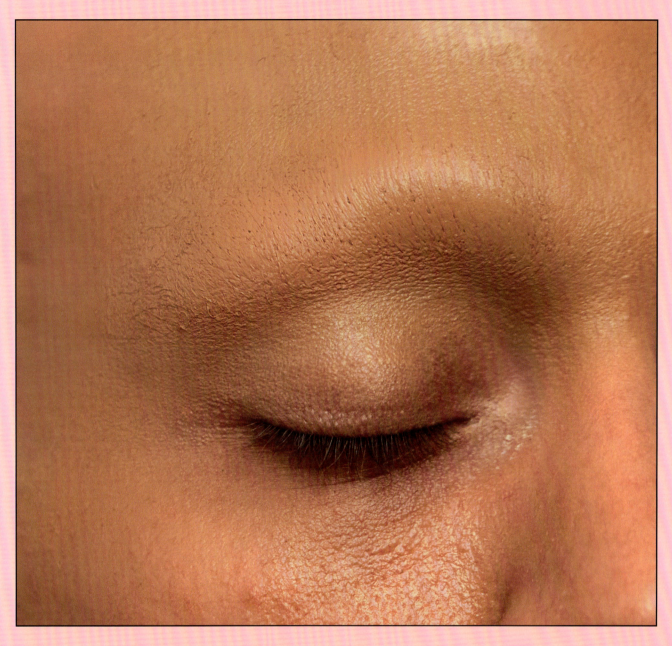

7 Repeat steps 18–21 from *Skill 4: Bald Cap*, p. 101, to finish.

SKILL 4

◊ **HOW TO CREATE A SCAR**

PREP STEP As usual, wipe the skin with **witch hazel** and clean it with **99% alcohol**.

1   For this skill, you will need an **alcohol paint palette**. Using a rose or blood tone and a **fine-tip brush**, delicately trace the desired shape of your scar onto the skin.

2   Use a **glue brush** to paint **Rigid Collodion** exactly where you applied the alcohol paint. Layer this a few times, drying the scar with a **blow dryer** in between coats.

3   If your subject is likely to be moving around, avoid wear and tear by adding a little **Pros-Aide** on top of the scar. Finish with **translucent powder**.

> The color you choose here depends on the age of the scar. Scars tend to whiten with age, whereas new scars are pinkish.

◊ HOW TO MAKE A FAKE PIMPLE USING A BALD CAP

1   Mix a dollop of **KY Jelly** with **methyl cellulose** and a **pigment** (rubber mask grease paint or acrylic paint work well) in the center of where you want to make your pimple, and glue a slightly larger section of bald cap around it.

2   Proceed with steps 15–21 from *Skill 4: Bald Cap*, p. 101.

3   Prick a hole in the center of the bald cap right before you shoot to create an exit for a realistically oozing pimple.

BALD

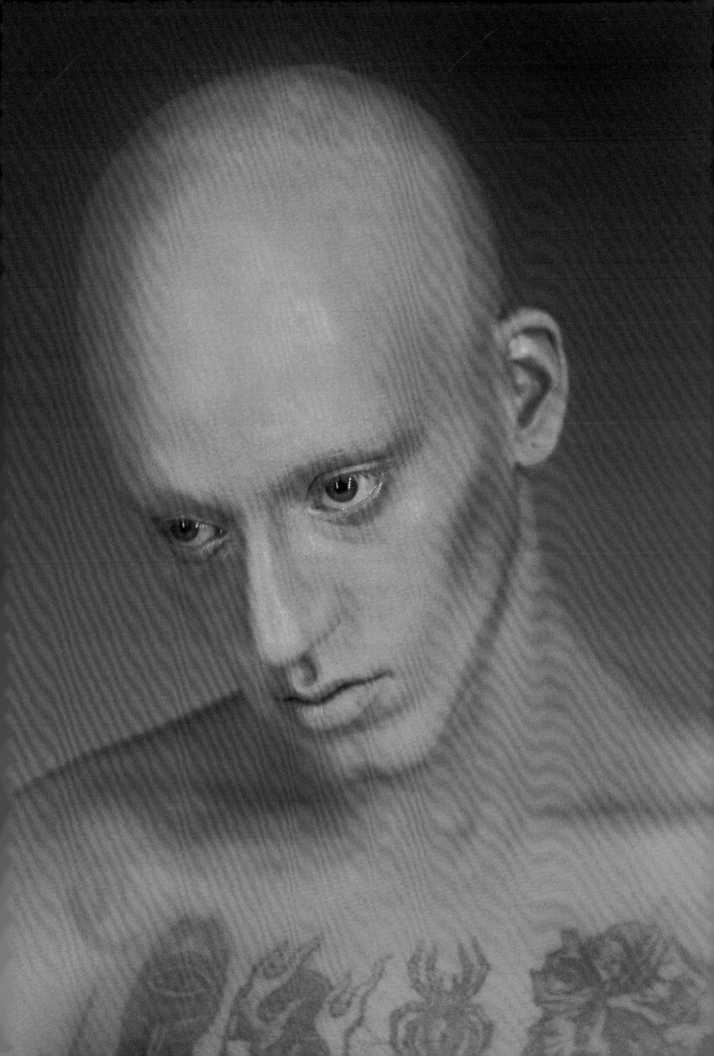

LOOK 4

NAME	Tripp
AGE	30
OCCUPATION	Musician
HOMETOWN	New York, NY

Using a **Ben Nye Hydra Sponge** and a **fine-tip brush** when needed, first apply **Kryolan Aquacolor in TV White** followed by **Pink**, and buff these into your first layer. To activate the Aquacolor, spray water directly into the pot.

Using the one-inch chip brush trick covered in *Skill 7: Cut*, p. 157, flick a liberal amount of Coral Adjuster from **Skill Illustrator's alcohol paint palette** over the entirety of the makeup. Applying this skin-tone color is how we create Tripp's pink tone.

Alcohol paints come in a palette version and a liquid version—we recommend using the liquid version for any airbrush effect because it is pre-thinned at the right consistency for that technique. (You can always get the same color in both versions.)

Continue the process of adding contours, buffing pink-tone cream paints from the **blush palette** with a **powder brush** in receding areas or areas you want to recede. (For more on these sculpting techniques, see *Skill 1b: III*, p. 53.)

ADDITIONAL TOOLS
- Ben Nye Hydra Sponge
- Fine-tip brush
- Kryolan Aquacolor in TV White and Pink
- Water spray bottle
- Alcohol paint palette in skin tones (we use Skin Illustrator)
- Blush palette
- Powder brush

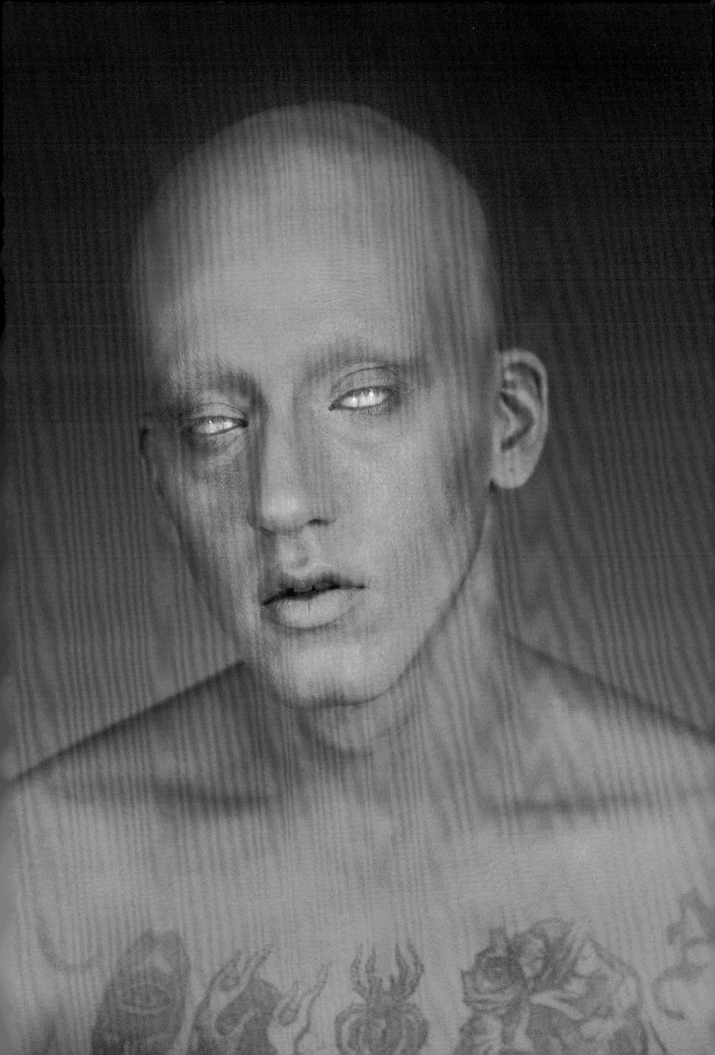

CHAPTER 5: HAIRY

Skill 5: Beard & Mustache Laying

TOOLS NEEDED	◊ Witch hazel
	◊ Cotton rounds
	◊ Crepe hair
	◊ Pros-Aide Cream
	◊ Wide tongue depressor
	◊ Red stipple sponge or latex-free foam wedge sponge
	◊ Rattail comb
	◊ Safety scissors
	◊ Lace mustache
	◊ Telesis 8 Matte Silicone Adhesive
	◊ Telesis 8 Adhesive Thinner
	◊ Mix holder
	◊ Glue brush

Hair is perhaps the most powerful way to indicate a character's private routines. In the script you see how a character treats the people in their life, but it is in their hair and makeup that you see how they treat themselves.

Who do they style themselves after? Are they seeking attention or anonymity? Perhaps their mom cuts their hair. How often do they wash it? Are they balding? Is it male pattern baldness or simply from stress? (Stress baldness is diffused over the entire head, while male pattern baldness follows the laterally receding hairline.)

In addition to personal style, hair also shows temporal progression. Stubble, for example, is an indication of the passage of time, a crucial continuity thread you must follow closely.

With the three simple lessons in this chapter, we will lay the groundwork for realistic beard laying, mustache application, and the dusting of days-old stubble.

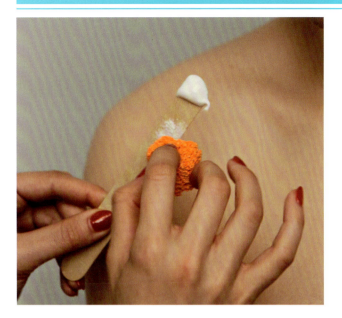 

1   First, prep the area of the skin where you will be applying the beard with **witch hazel** and **cotton rounds**. When working with **crepe hair**, it's important to keep both your working area and your fingers clean because it can easily—and quickly—get out of control. For this reason, begin by applying a dollop of **Pros-Aide Cream** onto a **wide tongue depressor**. This way, the hair will not contaminate the original container and you will have a surface on which to sponge off any excess glue you pick up in the process.

2   Now stipple the **sponge** on the area where you plan to lay the hair. Wait until it dries to clear. Please note that if your subject's hair doesn't match the crepe hair exactly, you may need to blend two different colors (see *How to Blend Hairs*, p. 131).

> You can make your own Pros-Aide Cream by stirring fumed silica powder (such as Cabosil) into liquid Pros-Aide. If you try this at home, we recommend doing this outside or in a well-ventilated room with an N95 surgical mask or respirator.

3 Lay the hair according to the illustration. The direction you lay the hair will ultimately dictate the shape of the beard. Using the metal tail of your **rattail comb**, or the back of your **safety scissors**, press down on the hair at the root along the top edge and gently pull down. (Apply more pressure if you want a thinner beard and less pressure if you want a thicker one.) Repeat this step over and over until the beard has filled out to your liking.

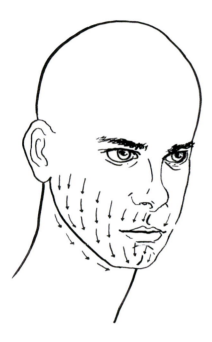

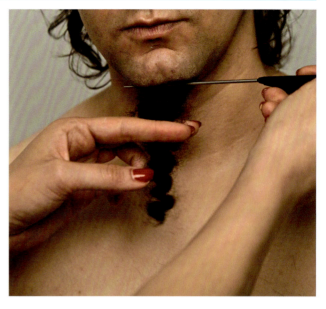

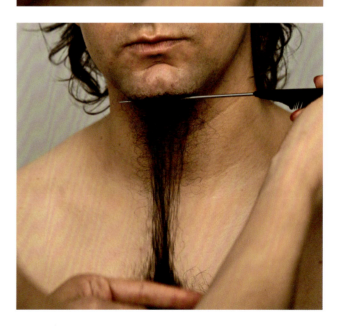

4   See *How to Create Stubble*, p. 131.

5   To prepare a **lace mustache**, first trim the lace around the hair roughly a quarter of an inch away from the knots. If you are going for a specific look, you can style the mustache prior to application. Regardless, you will probably want to reserve the option to trim it a little once it has been applied.

6   Pour one part **Telesis 8 Matte Silicone Adhesive** and one part **Telesis 8 Adhesive Thinner** into pot A of your **mix holder**, and pour only Telesis thinner into pot B. Use a **glue brush** to apply the glue from pot A to your subject's skin where you will apply the mustache, using the thinner from pot B to clean the brush as you go. You can also add a little more thinner directly to the glue if it gets too thick at any point. Let the applied glue dry, until tacky on the skin.

7   Apply the mustache. Telesis will adhere more efficiently when pressure is used, so make sure to press the lace into the applied glue with your rattail comb. Keep in mind that you can cut your mustache in half down the middle to have more control over the shape. This rule applies for any kind of facial hair addition—beards included—because every face is different and you may need to adapt placement accordingly.

> We use Telesis 8 Matte Silicone Adhesive on the lace pieces and Pros-Aide Cream on the crepe hair. Telesis, unlike Pros-Aide Cream, enables us to reuse lace because it can be cleaned by using 99% alcohol.

◊ HOW TO BLEND HAIRS

The key to crafting realistic hair? Highlights and lowlights.

1 Unravel your two strands of **crepe hair**, and hold them between your fingers. You want to tear each strand down the middle lengthwise so you have four strands total. Then take each half and tear those again. Repeat until you have a variety of strands of different colors. Hold the strands up and lightly comb them through. (Don't worry about hairballs—half of the hair will end up on the floor and you will finish with what feels like a very small amount. This is supposed to happen.)

2 After breaking apart the crepe hair and thinning it out, hold the hair perpendicular to your pointer and middle fingers and use **safety scissors** to cut a straight line. This is for application as well as finding your desired length.

Stack the two colors and continue to blend them until you arrive at your desired shade. For beards, begin with darker shades and layer lighter colors on top. This creates depth as you build the beard.

◊ HOW TO CREATE STUBBLE

Adding stubble is a useful technique for film continuity, and it helps to blend hair pieces as well.

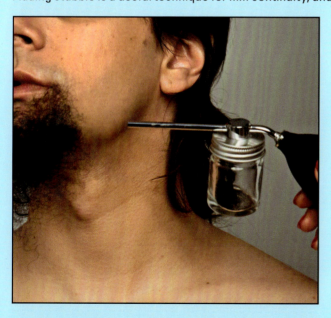
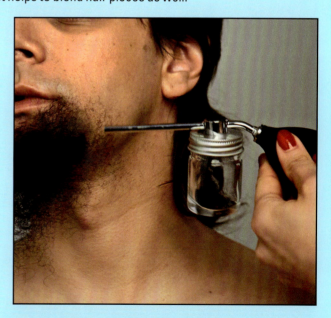

1 Trim a bundle of crepe hair into tiny pieces, essentially chopping it up—the finer, the better. It should look almost like dust. Put it into a **powder atomizer**. Apply **Pros-Aide** to the desired area of your subject's face with a **stipple sponge**.

2 Using your powder atomizer, gently pump the stubble onto the skin. Keep the nozzle moving so the stubble doesn't collect all in one place (unless you want it to).

HAIRY

NAME	Paul
AGE	32
OCCUPATION	Artist
HOMETOWN	Paris, FR

To achieve this blue, layer a **cream paint base in cerulean** with a **wedge sponge**. Continue layering with the same sponge as well as with a **powder puff** and **foundation brush**.

Once that layer sets, take a **liquid alcohol paint in yellow** and air-brush it all over. We use ProAiir Hybrid color, but as usual, if you don't have an **airbrush** you can use the chip brush flick technique (see *Skill 7: Cut*, p. 157). Use a **setting spray** to lock in the look.

The wig and mustache are both made out of lace, so we apply them using the same principles—with one difference. While we adhere the mustache with Telesis 8 Matte Silicone Adhesive, we use **Super Baldiez** for the wig because it's stronger, faster drying, and creates a particularly stretchy membrane for this complex look. Pros-Aide also works.

Flatten each piece of hair with the metal end of a **rattail comb** and dab it with a wet **kitchen towel** to remove the "glue shine." With the same adhesive, brush underneath the hair for added adherence. (Don't get too close to the hairline or it can appear gummy on camera.)

You can experiment with hair color without using dye. To blend the white facial hair, we simply brush more cerulean cream paint around the edges of the beard using a **mascara spoolie** dipped in paint.

Finally, we brush **liquid alcohol paint** on Paul's eyes, cheeks, and hair as blush. Since Paul's skin and hair are blue, we add contrast with a reddish hue (see *Color Theory*, p. 17). We then use a **powder brush** to dust on the highlights of the face and neck.

ADDITIONAL TOOLS	
	◊ Cream paint palette
	◊ Wedge sponge
	◊ Powder puff
	◊ Foundation brush
	◊ Liquid alcohol paint in yellow and red
	◊ Airbrush (or a modified one-inch chip brush for flicking)
	◊ Setting spray
	◊ Strong adhesive (we use Super Baldiez)
	◊ Rattail comb
	◊ Kitchen towel
	◊ Hair net
	◊ Mascara spoolie
	◊ Round powder brush

CHAPTER 6: BONY

Skill 6: Prosthetic Application

TOOLS NEEDED	◊ Witch hazel
	◊ Cotton rounds
	◊ Prosthetic piece (we use the Cyrano Nose from Rubber Wear)
	◊ 99% alcohol
	◊ Glue brush
	◊ Latex-free foam wedge sponges, including a torn wedge sponge
	◊ Pros-Aide
	◊ Translucent powder
	◊ Stomper brush
	◊ PAX paint in muscle layer color
	◊ Foundation
	◊ Foundation Brush

Exaggerated or unusual facial features (a dimple chin, for example) already look a bit like a prosthetic. When assessing the face of a subject awaiting creature makeup, cover their more ordinary features first, and then think about how to enhance the ones you first noticed when you saw them. This way, what is "fake" and what is "real" will be indiscernible.

Creatures are most persuasive when they have a basis in biology. Generally speaking, animals with close-set eyes make better predators. Overlapping visual fields create depth perception for the hunt. Prey creatures have eyes farther apart, resulting in stronger peripheral vision for detecting the threats that might surround them.

PREP STEP Prep the skin—in this case, the nose—with **witch hazel** and **cotton rounds** to remove oils that will inhibit the prosthetic's adherence.

1 Clean your **prosthetic piece** with **99% alcohol**, inside and outside, for the same reason. (If your prosthetic is pre-painted, avoid cleansing the painted side.)

> Typically, the prosthetics you make on your own will be gelatin or silicone, as you need a special oven for foam latex. However, there are places you can send your molds where they will professionally run them with foam latex on your behalf (see *Suppliers*, p. 178).

2 Using your **glue brush** or **latex-free foam wedge sponge**, apply **Pros-Aide** to your subject's nose (see *How to Apply a Tattoo*, p. 42). Place the prosthetic at the desired angle. Then, treating the appliance as a stencil, liberally dust **translucent powder** around it so you have a good idea of where the edges are going to land. This will leave an outline of your appliance and act as a guide.

3 Apply a thin layer of Pros-Aide to the inside of your prosthetic piece, being careful to avoid the edges. Let this dry clear.

4 Place the prosthetic right onto the tip of the nose. To achieve clean edges and secure placement, it's crucial for the central part of the piece to make contact first. If possible, flip the piece inside out to secure the center. Carefully (and patiently) run the glue brush along the inside edge. If you find some edges are flipped under or not laying properly, use 99% alcohol to release them, and reset.

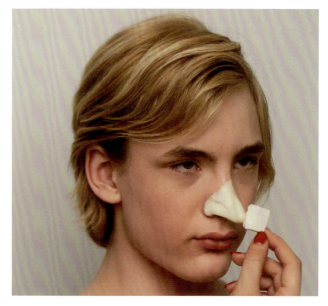

5 Once all of your edges are nicely adhered, take a corner of your **torn wedge sponge** (or any textured sponge of your choice) and dip it in Pros-Aide, sponging around the edge of the prosthetic and all over the piece itself. Not only does this help it adhere strongly to your subject, but it also creates a more even skin texture, helps the paint stick better, and seals the piece against moisture.

6   Using a **stomper brush**, apply translucent powder on top of the Pros-Aide along the edges of the piece. Apply firm pressure to the edges for the smoothest look. If you find you have a gap or a jump in the edge, you can use your Pros-Aide Cream (see *Skill 5: Beard & Mustache Laying*, p.125). You can think of its purpose here as equivalent to spackling. Wait for it to dry clear and press translucent powder on top.

7 With your torn wedge sponge, apply **PAX paint** to the nose in a muscle layer shade, such as a reddish coral. This shade helps to blend in and "take down" the color of the foam latex, so be sure to cover the entire prosthetic with a thin layer of paint, feathering out the edges.

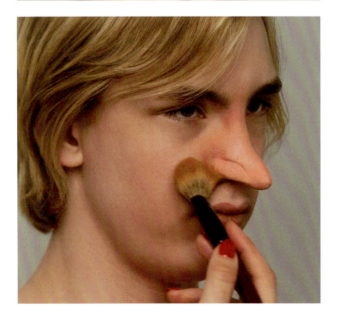

8   Apply the **foundation** of your choice over the PAX layer using a **foundation brush**.

> When it comes to certain facial features, it can be effective to lean into the muscle layer tone of your subject. In this case, the tip of the nose is often a little flushed, and the same goes for the tips of the ears, earlobes, and so on. This is why taking a step back and blending the edges of the prosthetic first is useful.

BONY

NAME	Augie
AGE	13
OCCUPATION	Middle school student
HOMETOWN	Glen Ridge, NJ

To make a monster out of Augie, we first clip his hair back in order to prepare the skin for prosthetic application. We apply **witch hazel** to his face and shoulders, followed by **barrier foam**, as he has particularly sensitive skin. We also clean the prosthetics inside and out with **99% alcohol**.

Next, we complete steps 1–9 in *Skill 6: Prosthetic Application*, p. 141, to apply a variety of **foam latex prosthetics** to Augie's face and body. These include arched brow covers, an aquiline nose ridge, a pointy elf nose, alien cheeks, and a pointed pixie chin. We also adapt two alien bone ridges intended for the top of the head to fit on Augie's shoulders. In general, don't worry too much about what store-bought prosthetics are technically intended for. Experimenting with your pieces can lead to unexpected uses and novel arrangements.

To paint Augie this softer, more pleasing shade of yellow, we begin by sponging a white paint all over his skin. This underpainting will diffuse the paint we layer on top, creating a deeper final tone. For this process, we use **Kryolan Aquacolor in TV White** and **Ben Nye's Hydra Sponge**, a round sponge that works well with water-activated paints.

Next, we add the yellow layer with **alcohol paint** and an **airbrush**, spraying a fine mist. If you're using the **one-inch chip brush** method instead, you can trim the bristles of the brush to create a similar flecked effect.

Then we spatter alcohol paint in Vein Tone and Coral Adjuster on top of the yellow to add dimension. To create the spattered effect, simply remove the airbrush's nozzle.

The key to rendering even the most fantastical creature creations as realistically as possible is to follow the same skills taught in *Skill 1a: Healthy*, p. 31, when it comes to the mucous membrane and color matching. The difference here is using **cream paint** and a **foundation brush** to create a uniform blue undertone on the lips, under the eyes, and at the tips of the prosthetic ridges (wherever the mucous membrane would show through). Following this same two-color philosophy is how you create a more coherent creature.

Next, we highlight with a **white pearlescent powder** just as we have done many times before: in the inner corners of the eyes, on the ridge of the nose, and on the collarbone.

Then, contour with a **gray contouring shade** from an eyeshadow palette. For help with placement, see the contouring lessons in *Skill 1b: III*, p. 53, particularly steps 7, 8, and 9, which show how even the most monstrous prosthetics can look like they're really part of the character's body.

For the finishing touches, set the surface using a **setting spray** like Ben Nye's Final Seal. Apply a thin layer of **KY Jelly** with the fingers and palms of the hand just like we have added moisturizer at the beginning of every lesson: this "sebum" is what makes Augie's final character look really alive. Finally, apply **fake eyelashes**: two at the top and one at the bottom of each eye.

ADDITIONAL TOOLS	
	◊ Witch hazel
	◊ Barrier foam
	◊ 99% alcohol
	◊ Foam latex prosthetics
	◊ Kryolan Aquacolor in TV White
	◊ Round yellow sponge (we use Ben Nye's Hydra Sponge)
	◊ Alcohol paint palette (we use Skin Illustrator)
	◊ Airbrush or one-inch chip brush
	◊ Cream paint palette
	◊ Foundation brush
	◊ White pearlescent powder
	◊ Gray contouring shade
	◊ Setting spray
	◊ KY Jelly
	◊ Fake eyelashes

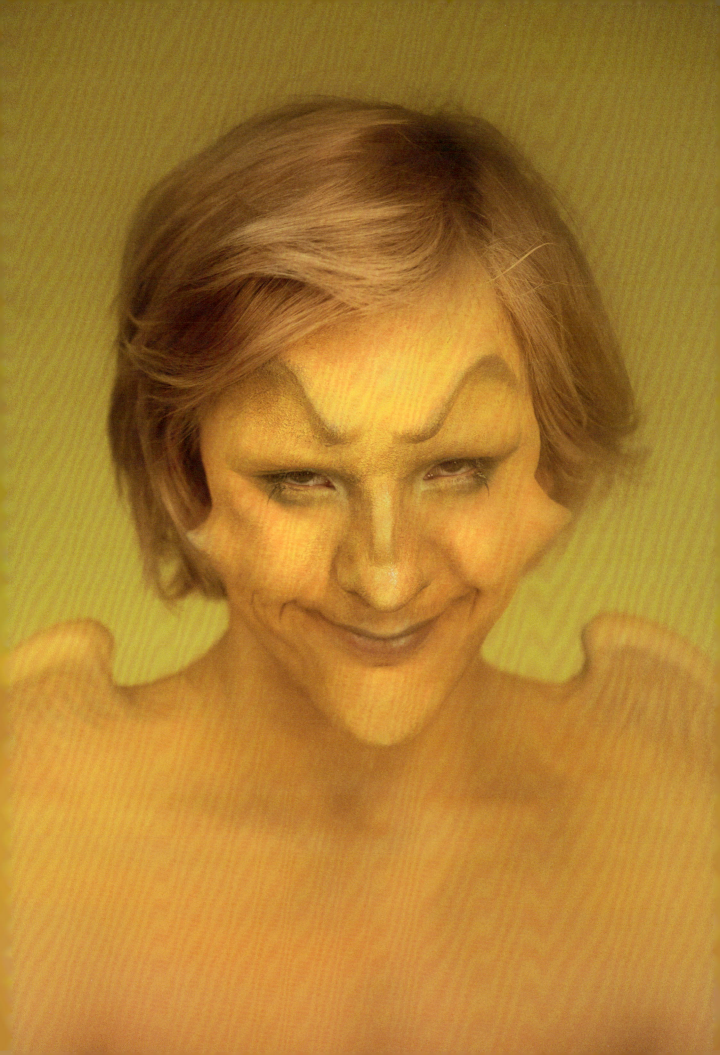

CHAPTER 7: BLOODY

Skill 7: Cut

TOOLS NEEDED	◊ Witch hazel
	◊ Cotton round
	◊ Metal spatula
	◊ 3rd Degree Silicone Modeling Compound
	◊ Metal palette
	◊ 99% alcohol
	◊ Tongue depressors
	◊ Concealer brush
	◊ Red stipple sponge
	◊ Angled tweezers
	◊ Pros-Aide Cream
	◊ Handheld fan
	◊ Alcohol paint palette in skin tones (we use Skin Illustrator in Complexion)
	◊ Fine-tip brush
	◊ One-inch chip brush
	◊ Work scissors (not safety scissors)
	◊ Gel-type blood (we use Reel Creations' Fresh Blood Gel)
	◊ Alcohol paint in Aged Blood shade

Making movies gives you the power to make a reality of your own. Blood is the proof. In life, blood drips and spurts when we have lost control. In movies, we can shape, color, and direct this most visceral of substances. To pull off dramatic blood work means that you have made the world fully manipulable.

First, you must place yourself in the middle of the action. Where was the subject standing in relation to the aggressor? Was the aggressor left-handed or right-handed? What made the cut? How long ago? How deep? It is a matter of forensic pathology.

This chapter contains lessons that will enable you to make scenes that are shocking yet grounded in reality.

CHAPTER 7

PREP STEP As usual, begin by using **witch hazel** and a **cotton round** to clean the skin and remove oils in your chosen area—choosing the area for the cut is crucial.

1 With your **metal spatula**, dispense **3rd Degree** onto your **metal palette** in parts A and B. Clean your spatula with **99% alcohol** between each dip. (You can also use two separate **tongue depressors** for this step, rather than the one spatula.) The goal is to not contaminate one pot with another, otherwise your entire jar may cure (and become useless).

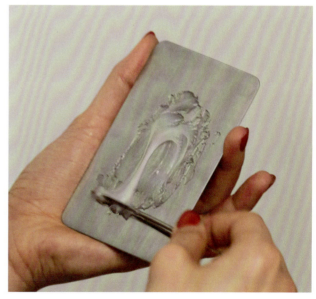

2 Mix the two dollops of 3rd Degree evenly. As you mix, scrape the bottom of the mixture in a whipping motion.

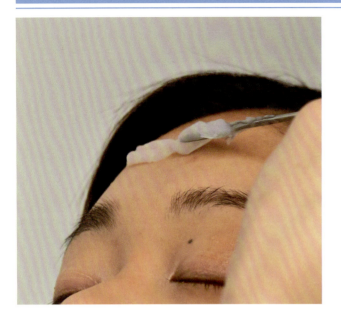

3   Lay the mixture on the area where you're making the cut, leaving some left over on the metal palette. Keep in mind that the mix will cure faster on skin (due to the body heat) and in a warm room.

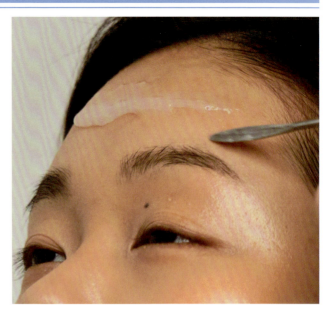

4   Apply 99% alcohol with the metal spatula to blend the edges. Make sure to keep a mass of excess in the center of where the cut will be. The more material you have here the deeper you can make the cut.

5   Blend further using 99% alcohol on a **concealer brush**.

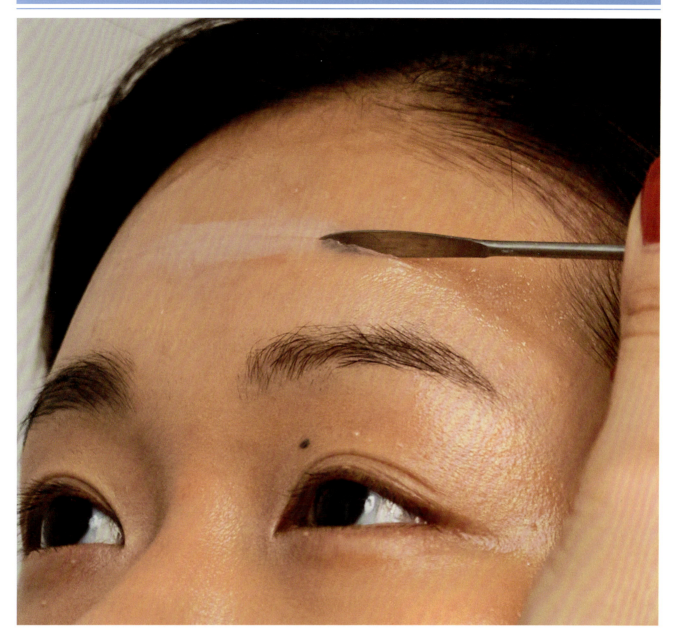

6   Using your metal spatula, test the leftover silicone on your metal palette to assess the cure time (we recommend waiting until it's about 50% cured so it retains its edges). Then cut a slit through the center of the silicone, using a slight wiggling motion to create an organically textured incision. Variation is your friend.

> Complete the sculpt in five minutes maximum. If you're in a hot room, or working with a subject who "runs hot," it will impact your working time. Alternatively, if you're working in a cold room, it may take longer for the silicone to cure. In some (rare) instances you may want to speed up the process with a blow dryer, but generally speaking this is a fight against the clock.

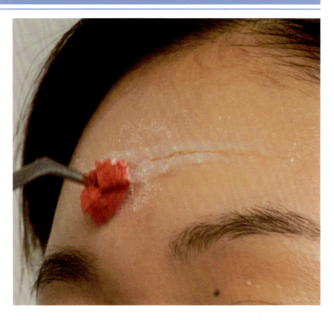

7   Take a small, torn-off piece of **red stipple sponge** (midway in texture between the white sponges and orange sponges you may have used so far). Spear this at the end of your **angled tweezers**. Meanwhile, add a dollop of **Pros-Aide Cream** to the end of a tongue depressor. Note: this is an especially important time to keep your fingers clean.

8   Stipple the Pros-Aide Cream on top of your cut. This will create a surface that can easily be painted. As a general rule, silicone only sticks to silicone, therefore paint will rub off if this layer is not applied. Use a **handheld fan** to dry the cut before moving on, or simply wait. Once dry, take an **alcohol paint palette in skin tones** and, with a **fine-tip brush**, add a wash to lightly tint the white cast caused by the silicone-based 3rd Degree.

9   Cut into a **one-inch chip brush** with **work scissors**. To make bristles of varying lengths, cut at an angle, keeping in mind that longer bristles create a fine mist and shorter bristles create a splattered effect. For airbrush users, it's the difference between taking the needle cap off or leaving it on. This is a key trick to fake an airbrush effect when you don't have one handy.

10   Dip the brush in your alcohol paint palette, choosing a color that closely matches the skin color of your subject, and flick this onto their skin.

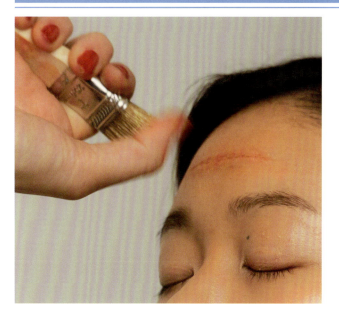

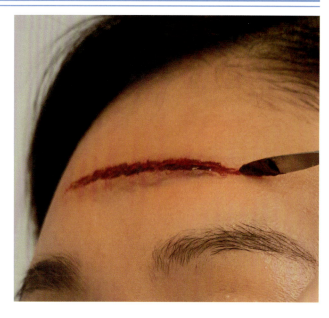

11 Continue this flicking technique with a mucous membrane-toned alcohol paint on a large chip brush. Alternatively, you can bounce paint directly against the skin. Continue to blend around the cut with the skin shade used at the end of step 8. Keep painting, alternating both layers of alcohol paints with brushing and flicking techniques. Bounce back and forth between colors until you find a balance that blends seamlessly into your subject's skin.

12 Using your metal spatula from before, fill in the slit you made with **gel-type blood**. Use the same motion you used to make the cut, wiggling the spatula as you go. The less perfect the line is, the more realistic the cut will appear.

13 To age the cut slightly, flick the **Aged Blood alcohol paint** shade using your customized chip brush.

> Always give a word of warning before you use this flicking technique. Make sure your subject's eyes are closed and that they are not breathing in while you work.

> This technique also serves as an ideal way to contour any prosthetics you may be using, as it helps cast realistic light and shade, depending on your angle.

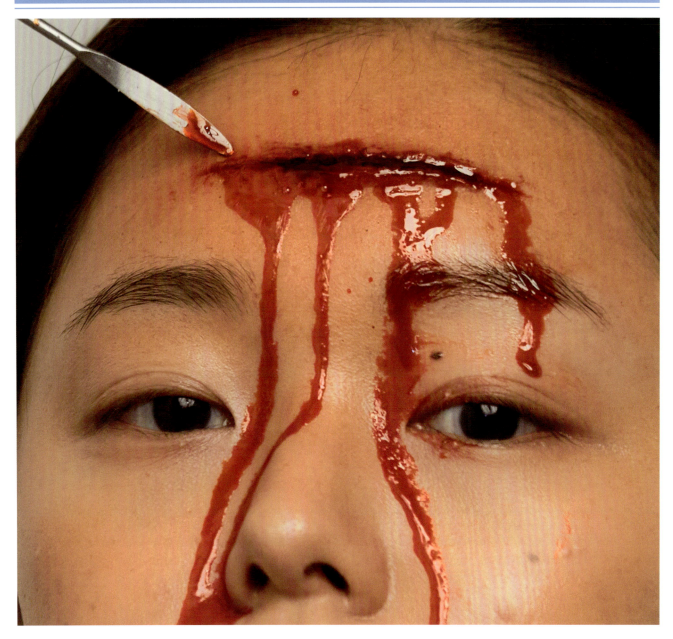

14 With the spatula, add more blood to create a realistic drip. You can also make scratches with miniscule movements of the spatula.

CHAPTER 7

◊ HOW TO MAKE A NECK BLADDER

TOOLS NEEDED

◊ Stencil
◊ Tape
◊ Black marker
◊ Liquid balloon latex
◊ CC cup
◊ Latex-free foam wedge sponges
◊ Q-tip
◊ Pros-Aide
◊ Party balloon, in a color close to your subject's skin tone
◊ Round powder brush
◊ Safety scissors

1 Place your neck-shaped **stencil** on a non-porous surface and **tape** it down.

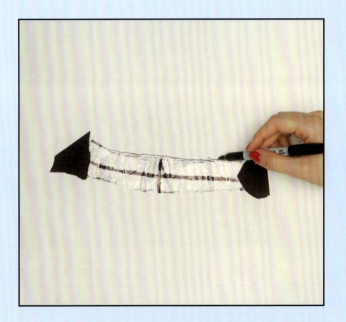

2 Take a **black marker** and outline the stencil. Then, remove the tape so you can outline at either end as well.

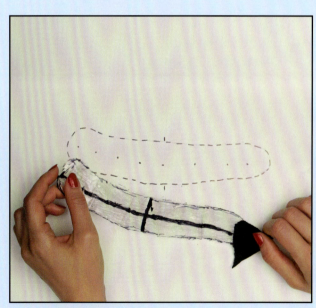

3 Remove the stencil.

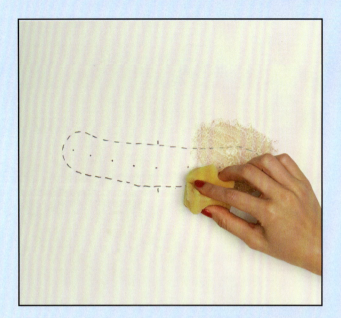 

4 Shake your bottle of **liquid balloon latex** before pouring it into a **CC cup**. With a **torn wedge sponge** that's cut in half, dab the latex just outside your outline. Once the first layer dries, repeat this step until you have applied three layers of liquid latex.

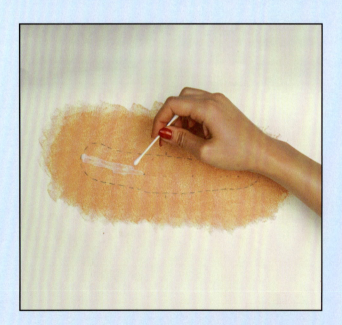 

5 Using a **Q-tip**, dab a line of **Pros-Aide** down the center of the latex and the length of your balloon. Let it dry.

6 Lay the **balloon** on its glued side, all the way down the stencil.

CHAPTER 7

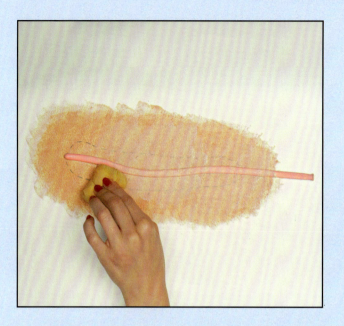

7 Repeat step 4 until you have applied another three layers of liquid latex.

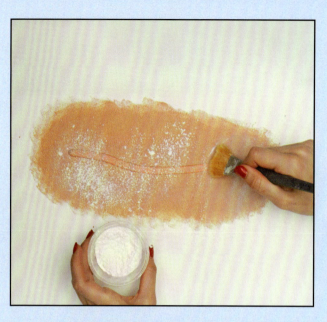

8 Apply powder along the length of your bladder with a **round powder brush**, using a sprinkle-and-tap movement.

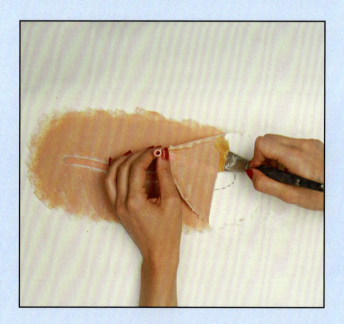

9 Peel the bladder up gently, using your powder brush to get underneath the edges and coax it up as you lift bit by bit.

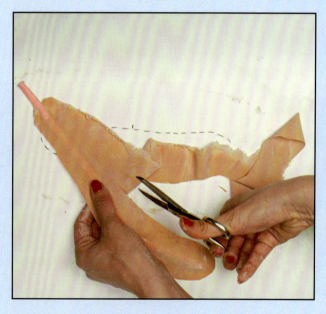

10 Trim the bladder just outside the dotted lines with **scissors**.

◊ HOW TO APPLY A NECK BLADDER

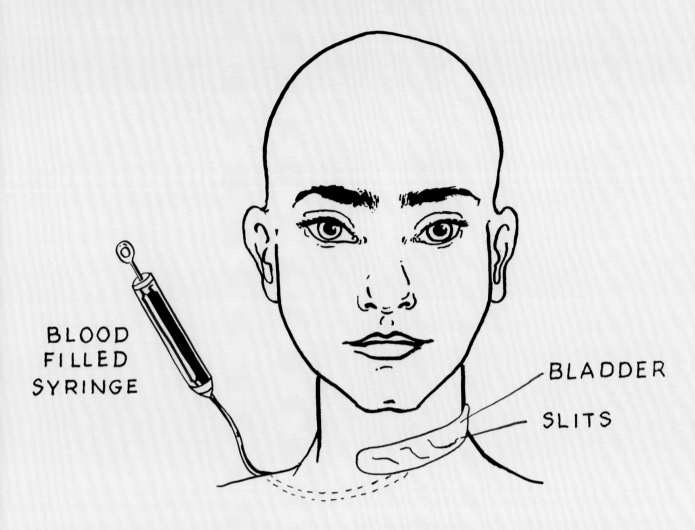

Now you have a squib you can apply directly to your subject's neck.

First prepare the skin with an **astringent** and apply a **barrier foam**. Then apply **liquid latex** to the area to which you'll attach the squib. Apply another layer of liquid latex to the side of the squib that will be pressed against your subject's skin. Wait for both to dry to mostly clear and then press them together. Apply a layer of liquid latex around the edges of the squib to blend, and then powder as usual.

The squib can be placed under a prosthetic or under clothing. Line up your prosthetic and cut into the top side of the balloon, using safety scissors to dictate the blood flow.

Insert **plastic tubing a half-inch in diameter** through the balloon's opening and use a **pesticide sprayer, bike pump**, or **large syringe** to create your blood movement for the camera.

> It is important to determine the camera frame for this effect. If it is a closeup, you will be able to stand very close to the subject and thereby have more control over the amount of blood that you release. You may even be able to pump directly into the balloon. If it is a medium or long shot, you will need more tubing and a place to hide.

◊ BLOOD TYPES

There are a wide variety of fake bloods available to purchase, but when choosing the right one for your purposes you will need to consider different factors, such as:

◊ the origin and the age of the wound you're creating

◊ the area of the body or fabric on which you're going to apply the blood

◊ the camera lighting of the scene, which can alter how the blood appears

In general, darker tones look the most realistic, if that's what you're going for.

Some of our favorites fake bloods include:

Blood capsule
Safe to use in the mouth, these are powder capsules that react with saliva if you bite into them.

Flavored blood
If you're going to douse your subject in blood, it might as well taste pleasant. We like Ben Nye's classic Stage Blood in Zesty Mint.

Hershey's Chocolate Syrup
When shooting in black-and-white, the best fake blood is simply Hershey's. It makes a starker contrast than red blood and has a similar consistency.

Methyl cellulose
A common thickener made from wood pulp used for blood work and mold-making, methyl cellulose is used in film to mimic slime, oil, saliva, semen, and sweat. Because it's completely edible, it's also widely used for making bloody drool.

Thick blood
A fake blood marked as "thick blood" will usually be a gel-like blood, great for creating fresh-looking wounds. Its thicker, gelatinous consistency also allows for greater malleability and working time (we like Ben Nye's best).

Thinned blood
This fake blood is typically diluted with water to facilitate spraying or pumping and avoid clogging in the rig.

Always talk to the wardrobe department about what kind of blood you're going to use, because some blood stains and others don't.

BLOODY

NAME	Minami
AGE	24
OCCUPATION	Dancer
HOMETOWN	Hiroshima, JP

We start by using a **comb** to saturate the hair with **hair gel,** so the **fake blood** has a base to land on.

For the eyes, we use an **eyeliner brush** with **black cream eyeliner** on Minami's upper lash line and make a slight wing. With the same color, we extend the eyebrows toward her hairline. We then add **fake eyelashes**: two on the top and one on the outer corner of the bottom lashes.

Light lip contouring can lend the mouth a more defined shape without introducing a new color. Using the same eyeliner brush and some of our **red lipstick**, we trace the corners of her mouth and the Cupid's bow, and finish by drawing a vertical line down the center of the upper and lower lips.

To protect Minami from all the fake blood we're about to douse her with, we apply **barrier foam** on her body. This prevents the skin from staining pink. (We also cover the floor with a plastic tarp.)

We pour the fake blood on Minami once she's positioned in front of the camera, using a **one-inch chip brush** to guide the way.

Fake blood is water-soluble. To maintain its fresh look and prevent it from developing a film on top, we periodically rewet the bloody areas with our **water spray bottle**. This is a good trick to keep the blood looking fresh without wasting product. We keep damp **paper towels** on hand to wipe away any stray blood.

ADDITIONAL TOOLS	
	◊ Comb
	◊ Hair gel
	◊ Fake blood
	◊ Eyeliner brush
	◊ Black cream eyeliner
	◊ Fake eyelashes
	◊ Red lipstick
	◊ Barrier foam
	◊ One-inch chip brush
	◊ Water spray bottle
	◊ Paper towels

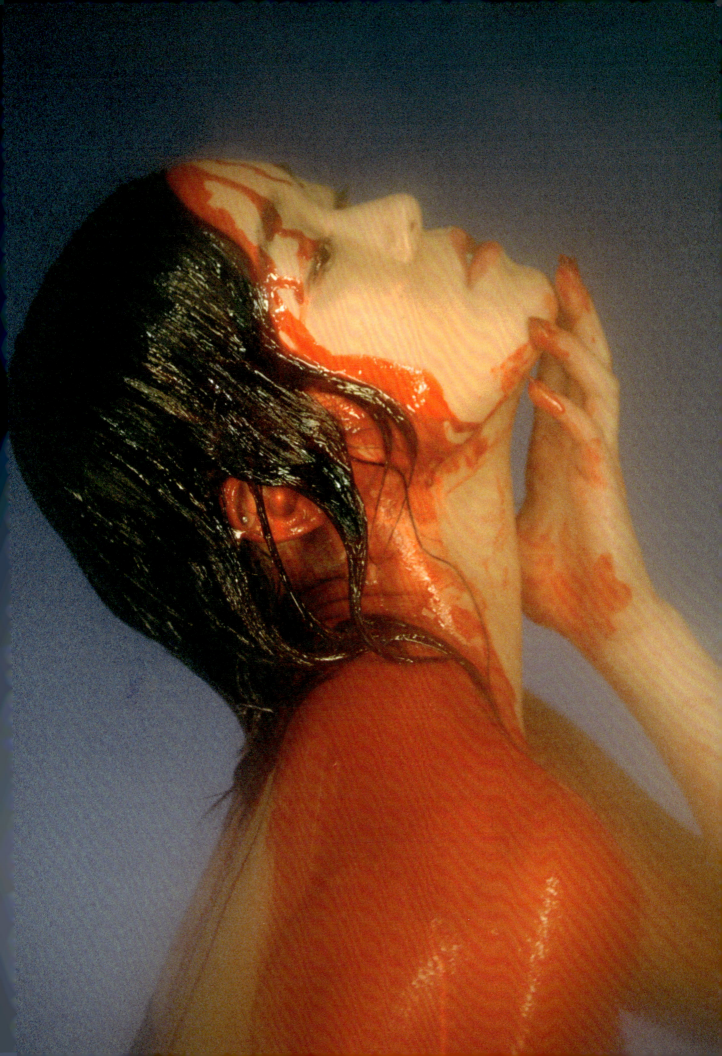

GLOSSARY

3rd Degree
A two-part silicone modeling compound for creating scars, deep cuts, and burns, either applied directly to the skin or cured in a mold.

Cupid's bow
The center of the upper lip where its two peaks meet (named after the bow of Cupid, the Roman god of erotic love).

Flashing
The excess plastic of the bald cap (or silicone prosthetic appliance) that you ease away—or "burn"—with acetone, melting the edges into the skin.

Mucous membrane
Body "openings" such as your lips, genitals, nipples, and the waterline of your eyelids share a color tone dictated by your mucous membrane. Studying this tone reveals the natural color palette of a person's body and is therefore crucial in selecting the right shade of blush. (Monsters have mucous membranes too; see *Look 6: Bony*, p. 148.)

Muscle layer
We refer to the color of the muscle that lies right under the skin for blending foam latex pieces and bald caps.

Nasolabial folds
The folds in the skin between the nose and the corners of the mouth.

Orbital bone
The spherical bone that houses the eye socket.

PAX paint
An opaque, long-lasting paint flexible enough to adhere to latex. PAX paint was originally developed by makeup artist Dick Smith in order to prevent foam latex from degrading (see *Skill 6: Prosthetic Application*, p. 141). You can buy it or make your own by mixing one part Pros-Aide with one part acrylic paint.

Pros-Aide
A water-based glue that dries to a water-resistant adhesive. Pros-Aide was originally a medical adhesive, and is now used in special effects makeup.

Pros-Aide Cream
A thicker version of Pros-Aide. Unlike the liquid version, its texture allows for a denser application, which is especially useful for hair laying. Also referred to in some circles as Bondo or matted Pros-Aide.

Stipple (v.)
A technique used to create realistic skin texture by applying a substance with a bouncing motion. A textured sponge is typically used to mimic the appearance of skin texture.

Stipple (n.)
A makeup product applied to stretched skin to create the appearance of wrinkles.

T-zone
The area in the middle of the face—the forehead, nose, and chin—where skin tends to be more active and oily, leading to blemishes like blackheads.

SUPPLIERS

1 Alcone Company
5-45 Forty-Ninth Ave.
Long Island City, NY 11101
800-466-7446
alconemakeup.com

Among other general makeup supplies, they carry the inexpensive rubber wear prosthetics we use in *Look 6: Bony*, p. 148.

2 Manhattan Wardrobe Supply
245 W 29th St. 8th floor
New York, NY 10001
212-268-9993
wardrobesupplies.com

3 Frends Beauty
5244 Laurel Canyon Blvd.
North Hollywood, CA 91607
818-769-3834
frendsbeauty.com

4 Kikko Import
825 Sixth Ave.
New York, NY 10001

Emporium of premade wigs and hair pieces

5 Johnblakeswigs.com
855-452-9447

Lace hair pieces for all types of hair (wig, beard, side burns etc.)

6 Motion Picture F/X Company
2920 W. Magnolia Blvd.
Burbank, CA 91505
818-563-2366
motionpicturefx.com

For an industry standard advanced option, RBFX prosthetics are available here and come highly recommended. With the full catalog of pieces available online, they will also fill your molds if you make a custom piece.

7 National Fiber Technology, Inc.
15 Union St.
Lawrence, MA 01840
978-686-2964
nftech.com

Great resource for spandex fur for any creature designs.

FURTHER READING

Anselmo, Stefano. *Il trucco e la maschera*. Milan: BCM, 1997.

Aucoin, Kevyn. *Face Forward*. New York: Little, Brown and Company, 2000.

Aucoin, Kevyn. *Making Faces*. New York: Little, Brown and Company, 1997.

Bandy, Way. *Designing Your Face: An Illustrated Guide to Using Cosmetics*. New York: Random House, 1977.

Bandy, Way. *Styling Your Face: An Illustrated Guide to Fifteen Cosmetic Face Designs for Women and Men*. New York: Random House, 1981.

Baygan, Lee. *Techniques of Three-Dimensional Makeup*. New York: Watson-Guptill Publications, 1982.

Berger, Howard, and Marshall Julius. *Masters of Make-Up Effects: A Century of Practical Magic*. London: Welbeck Publishing, 2022.

Brown, Bobbi. *Bobbi Brown Makeup Manual: For Everyone from Beginner to Pro*. New York: Grand Central Life & Style, 2008.

Brown, Bobbi, and Annemarie Iverson. *Bobbi Brown Beauty: The Ultimate Beauty Resource*. New York: William Morrow, 1997.

Buchman, Herman. *Stage Makeup*. New York: Watson-Guptill Publications, 1971.

Corson, Richard. *Stage Makeup*. New York: F. S. Crofts & Company, 1942.

Fox, Charlie. *This Young Monster*. London: Fitzcarraldo Editions, 2017.

Kehoe, Vincent J-R. *Special Make-Up Effects*. Abingdon, UK: Focal Press, 1991.

Place, Stan Campbell. *The Art and Science of Professional Makeup*. Albany, NY: Milady, 1990.

Savini, Tom. *Grand Illusions: Book I / Bizarro! A Learn-by-Example Guide to the Art and Technique of Special Make-Up Effects*. Charlotte & Los Angeles: Imagine Inc. and Morris Costumes, 1983 / New York: Harmony Books, 1984.

Savini, Tom. *Grand Illusions: Book II*. Charlotte & Los Angeles: Morris Costumes, 1996.

Smith, Dick. *Do-It-Yourself Monster Make-Up Handbook*. New York: Warren Publishing Company, 1965.

Taylor, Al, and Sue Roy. *Making a Monster: The Creation of Screen Characters by the Great Makeup Artists*. New York: Crown Publishers, 1984.

Beauty of the Beast
A Makeup Manual
By Emily Schubert

A24 Films LLC
New York, NY
a24films.com

Head of Publishing
Perrin Drumm

Publishing Operations Manager
Shayan Saalabi

Editor
Claire Marie Healy

Copy Editors
Lauren Hooker
Zachariah DeGiulio

Toolkit Illustrations
John Burgoyne

Face Illustrations
Daniel Obzejta

Thank You
Alex Bag
Alex Traub
David Levine
Doreen St. Félix
Ethan Young
Isabella Achenbach
John Paul Lopez-Ali
Jordu Schell
Kazu Hiro
Keith Edmier
Nick Harwood
The Schubert Family
Zoe Beyer

Design Concept
Chris Wu, Nazlı Ercan,
Wkshps

Typefaces
Univers and Apollo
designed by Adrian Frutiger

Paper
Fedrigoni Splendorlux
2 HB 350gsm, and Condat matt
Périgord 130 gsm

Printer
Conti Tipocolor, Italy

Photo Production

Creative Direction & Makeup Artist
Emily Schubert

Makeup
Christalla Elizabeth
Izzi Galindo
Jackie Zbuska

Photographer
Jason Al-Taan

Production
Paradise Productions

Executive Producer
Jill Ferraro

Production Managers
Jenny Slattery
Mia Jarrett

Additional Production Support
Justine Newman

Talent
August Bag
Kalifa
Minami Ando
Nat Carlson
Paul Gondry
Samantha Grace Landrum
Stephen Gurewitz
Theda Palmer Saxton
Tripp Jones

Casting Directors
Eléonore Hendricks
Elise Raven
Salome Oggenfuss

Set Design
Elysia Belilove

Hair Stylist
Issac Davidson

Wardrobe
Holly McClintock

Post Production Supervisor
Gregory Wikstrom

Lighting Director
William Takahashi

Lighting Assistant
Matt Roady

Key Production Assistant
Fernando Osorio

Production Assistants
Camey Falcone
Enrique Raxach
Jos Howard Demme

©2024 the authors, editors, and owners of all respective content.

All rights reserved; no part of this publication may be reproduced, stored in a retrieval system, or transmitted in any form or by any means, electronic, mechanical, photocopying, recording, or otherwise, without prior written consent of the publisher.

Every effort has been made to identify copyright holders and obtain their permission for the use of copyrighted material. The publisher apologizes for any errors or omissions and would be grateful if notified at publishing@a24films.com of any corrections that should be incorporated in future reprints or editions of this book.

ISBN 978-1-960078-05-6